FAITH

FAITH

TAKING GOD AT HIS WORD

MORRIS H. CHAPMAN

BROADMAN PRESS
NASHVILLE, TENNESSEE

© Copyright 1992 • Broadman Press
4253-54
0-8054-5354-7

Dewey Decimal Classification: 234.2
Subject Heading: FAITH
Library of Congress Catalog Card Number: 92-14185
Printed in the United States of America

Unless otherwise indicated, all Scripture references are from the *King James Version*. Scripture quotations marked NASB are from the *New American Standard Bible*. © The Lockman Foundation, 1960, 1962, 1963, 1968, 1971, 1972, 1973, 1975, 1977. Used by permission.

Library of Congress Cataloging-in-Publication Data

Chapman, Morris.
    Faith / Morris H. Chapman.
       p. cm.
    ISBN 0-8054-5354-7
    1. Faith—Biblical teaching. I. Title.
    BS680.F27C48 1992
    234'.2—dc20
                                    92-14185
                                           CIP

Acknowledgments

My deepest thanks to my present-day heroes of the faith:

Some are pastors, some evangelists, others teachers. Still others are members of congregations I have been privileged to pastor . . .

First Baptist Church, Rogers, Texas
First Baptist Church of Woodway, Waco, Texas
First Baptist Church, Albuquerque, New Mexico
First Baptist Church, Wichita Falls, Texas.

Church members who have been my constant encouragers in the faith,

My secretary, *Barbara Schaefer,* who typed the manuscript for this book. Her strong faith, level head, incredible skills, and caring spirit make her the perfect pastor's secretary,

My wife, *Jodi,* and our children *Chris* and *Stephanie.* My favorite daughter-in-law *Reneé* and my favorite son-in-law, *Scott.* Each one walks by faith and has brought a special joy into my life.

Preface

This book, *FAITH* (with the subtitle of *Taking God at His Word*), has been a "magnificent obsession" of mine throughout my ministry. The subject has seized my heart and mind until I finally *had to let it out!*

Faith is the key doctrine in our relationship with God the Father, God the Son, and God the Holy Spirit. Faith in Jesus Christ is, as explained throughout, the only way to salvation and eternal life. At its simplest, I feel, faith is believing God, trusting Him, accepting Him at face value—yes, taking Him at His Word. Faith is counting on God not only for salvation—but for all of life.

Why another book when there are many on the market? I have had a Holy-Spirit-instilled conviction over the years to share this material, praying that somehow my studies might bless and strengthen fellow believers who are indeed up against the forces of Satan in a predominantly faithless generation. I have fitfully prayed and wrestled with the material which centers around verses in the great faith chapter, Hebrews 11, and corresponding Scriptures in Genesis, Exodus, and two verses in Jude.

Abel, Enoch, Noah, Abraham, and Moses are paraded before us as heroes of the faith—as those who took God at His word—but who also, even as we, faltered and failed until being revived by a resurgent faith in God.

Every Christian has the potential, in his or her own right, of being a hero of the faith for the Lord Jesus Christ. Awesome is perhaps an overused, even abused, word, but it comes close to describing our emotions as we "stand amazed in the presence of Jesus the Nazarene," and we can only do that through faith. Through faith we are able to know the unknowable, hear the unhearable, plumb the depths of God's revelation, and even to see the invisible.

May the Holy Spirit light up your life as we are awed by the magnitude of faith and how it can continue to transform our lives.

—Morris H. Chapman

Contents

Preface vii

1. There's No Other Way But This 11
   Hebrews 11:4; Genesis 4:1-8

2. Walking with God 27
   Hebrews 11:5; Genesis 5:24; Jude 14-15

3. Rising Above the Flood 39
   Hebrews 11:7; Genesis 6:1-16

4. Taking God at His Word 55
   Hebrews 11:8; Genesis 12:1

5. Stop Trying—Start Trusting......................................69
   Hebrews 11:8; Genesis 12:1-4

6. Finding God's Way 83
   Hebrews 11:8-10; Genesis 12:1-3,17:5

7. Living in the Faith Dimension 93
   Hebrews 11:9-10

8. When Faith Falters 107
   Hebrews 11:8-10; Genesis 11:31-32

9. Famine or Feast? 125
   Genesis 12:10; 13:1-10

10. Fulfillment in the Family 137
    Genesis 21:1-14

11. Turning Your Back on the World..........................149
    Hebrews 11:23-29

12. About Faith: Forward March 163
    Hebrews 11:27-29; Exodus 8:25-32; 10:8-10,23-29

1.

There's No Other Way But This

Hebrews 11:4; Genesis 4:1-8

*By faith Abel offered unto God a more
excellent sacrifice than Cain, by which he
obtained witness that he was righteous, God
testifying of his gifts: and by it he being
dead yet speaketh.* Hebrews 11:4

Hebrews 11 is often referred to as "God's Hall of Faith." Human beings have tried every conceivable way to reach heaven, but the Bible declares, "There is only one way" (see John 14:6 and Acts 4:12). Verse 4 states, "By faith, Abel offered unto God a more excellent sacrifice than Cain, by which he obtained witness that he was righteous. God testifying of his gifts and by it, he being dead, yet speaketh." Abel left a living legacy.

The writer of Hebrews tells us how to worship. He points us to an account from Genesis 4 in the Old Testament. Even there the message was: faith, the way of the cross, leads home. "There's no other way but this." You may ask "Do you mean that even in the fourth chapter of Genesis, where there is the story of Cain and Abel, that the Word of God taught the way of the cross?"

Absolutely, for the story of Cain and Abel, those two sons of Adam and Eve, reveals that God alone is to be worshiped. The story also speaks about the right way to worship and the wrong way to worship.

Jesus said, "God is a spirit, and they that worship him, must worship him in spirit and in truth." Many people worship God, but they are not in the Spirit. And some people worship God, but their worship is not according to the truth of God's Word.

Many have the idea that they can merely come to a house of worship and can only pretend to be worshiping. If they told the truth, they would have to confess, "Oh, I believe there's a God, but I really put no faith in Him. I'm just going through the motions." And they somehow believe they can go through the motions of worship for most of their lives and be obedient to God.

But the Bible teaches that there is a right way to worship, and that way to worship is to be in the Spirit, and to worship according to the truth of God's Word.

How many people come to church on Sunday morning, giving practically no thought to what is really going to occur in the hour of worship? How many, when they arise on Sunday morning, make time really to pray for the power of God to fall upon that service?

How many people consciously pray, "Dear Lord Jesus, I know that someone there this morning is going to be lost. I know that if they would die right now, they'd go to hell and not to heaven. Dear Lord, I pray that as the Holy Word of God is opened and preached with clarity, that the unsaved will plead, 'God, I'm a sinner, and I'm in need of a Savior'"? How many pray before and during the service, "Oh, God, come in power and conviction, and bring conversion to those who're without Christ"?

So, many folks do not worship God as He intends to be worshiped. When we approach worship we should begin to plan days ahead saying "Lord, as I come, I want to open your Word and pray for you to illumine your Word to my heart."

Two Men and Two Approaches to Worship

I must needs go home by the way of the Cross
There's no other way but this;
I shall ne'er get sight of the gates of light
If the way of the Cross I miss.

—Jessie Brown Pounds

The words of that old hymn have always held the key—in both Old and New Testaments. In Genesis 4 . . .

God presents the account of these two men, who came to worship the Lord. "Cain was a tiller of the ground," the Bible says. He worshiped the Lord by bringing his produce as an offering to God. Abel was a keeper of sheep. He worshiped God by offering a lamb as a sacrifice to God.

Hebrews 11:4 refers to Abel, but has nothing about Cain. Why? Because Abel worshiped God righteously and Cain did so wrongfully.

Two Methods of Religion

"Cain was the founder of the world's first false religion, a religion which is at the heart of all false religions ever since. Essentially, Cain's religion was one of good works and human merit. According to him, salvation must be earned; he must pay the price. He offered to God the fruit of the earth, the product of his labors, the sweat of his brow, his toil and self-effort. His religion is summed up in Scripture as 'the way of Cain' (Jude 11) and is rejected, root and branch, by God. It ignored Calvary and the shedding of blood."[1]

That verse says, "By faith Abel offered unto God a more excellent sacrifice than Cain, by which he obtained witness that he was righteous, God testifying of his gifts: and by it he being dead yet speaketh." I believe Abel was the first man of faith. You might remark, "He was not the first man to live on the earth, so how is it that he was the first man of faith? He was not the first man that fellowshiped with God, either."

Of course, Cain did not respond in faith, and that leaves Adam and Eve, but Adam and Eve had no need of faith until they sinned. They had lived in an intimate fellowship with God. Even after they sinned, they still had the memory of that unique relationship with their Creator. In the fullest sense, their children, Cain and Abel, were the first ones to have need of faith.

Two verses later the Bible says, "But without faith it is impossible to please him, for he that cometh to God must believe that He is, and that he is a rewarder of them that diligently seek him."

So a person must come to God by faith, faith in God's Son, the Lord Jesus Christ, as personal Savior. There's no other way but this. Jesus did not mince words but plainly put it: "I am the way, the truth, and the life: no man cometh unto the Father, but by me" (John 14:6). So Jesus Christ is not a way to God. Jesus Christ is not even the best way to God, Jesus Christ is *the only way* to God.

The Only Way

He alone is the Way, the Truth, and the Life. He is the Door. He is the only avenue to eternal life, the kingdom of God, and heaven. He is the all-sufficient One. He is King of kings and Lord of lords. Without Him mankind is doomed to an eternal residence in the fires of hell. Without Him all is dark, dim, hopeless, horrible, and indescribably terror-filled.

"And Adam knew Eve his wife, and she conceived, and bare Cain, and said I have gotten a man from the Lord" (Gen. 4:1).

In the Hebrew, Cain means "I have acquired him or I have asked him of the Lord." God had promised Adam and Eve a deliverer. Perhaps Eve believed that Cain was going to be the deliverer, and of course, she was mistaken.

"And she again bare his brother Abel" (v. 2a). Abel means "vanity," "breath," or "vapor." His name seems literally to be a prophecy of the brevity of his life. "And Abel was a keeper of sheep, but Cain was a tiller of the ground." (v. 2b).

"And in process of time it came to pass, that Cain brought of the fruit of the ground an offering unto the Lord. And Abel, he also brought the firstlings of his flock and of the fat thereof. And the Lord had respect unto Abel and to his offering. But unto Cain and to his offering he had not respect" (vv. 3-5a). God was pleased with the offering of Abel, but he did not accept the offering of Cain.

"And Cain was very wroth [he was very angry], and his

countenance fell. And the Lord said unto Cain, Why art thou wroth? and why is thy countenance fallen? If thou doest well, shall thou not be accepted? and if thou doest not well, sin lieth at the door. And unto thee shall be his desire, and thou shalt rule over him. (v. 5a-7).

Every moment a person is living in disobedience of God, he can be assured that sin, like a hound, lies at his door. Some scholars feel that the Hebrew may mean "sin offering." Whatever, sin lies at the door, but the sin offering is also available.

And God said to Cain, "Why, sin lies at the door as long as you are disobedient in your worship." "And unto thee shall be his desire and thou shalt rule over him. And Cain talked with Abel his brother: and it came to pass, when they were in the field [and the Septuagint literally says, "Let us go into the field," as if Abel were enticed into the field by Cain] that Cain rose up against Abel his brother, and slew him" (vv. 7c-8).

Lessons from Abel and Cain

C. I. Scofield once observed: "The difference between the Atonement as set forth in the Old Testament and as presented in the New is that in the former case the sheep died for the shepherd; in the latter the Shepherd died for the sheep."

What do we learn from the worship of the second and third men who lived on the earth? I feel we learn that men worship God in one of two fashions. There is a difference between religion and salvation. Many people have religion but do not have salvation. Religion is what a person does for himself. If a person comes to the house of God believing that his goodness will spare him from hell, that God's going to have mercy on him because of his goodness, he has missed the entire purpose of Christ's sacrifice. Unregenerate human beings boast, "I'm going to be saved, but I'm going to do it my way." Sounds like a song, doesn't it? I believe that was exactly Cain's attitude. He did it his way.

Cain worshiped God by his good works, but Abel worshiped Him by faith.

Cain, no doubt, was a hardworking farmer. He plowed, planted, cultivated, harvested. Under the hot sun he toiled day after day. And when he came to worship, Cain no doubt offered the biggest and best of his labor, the most luscious fruit, the most succulent vegetables. He may have declared, "Nothing but the best." But the Bible reports that "God had no respect for his offering." He would not accept it. Why? Because, our best, in the wrong spirit, is not enough. We are saved, not by doing good works but by God's grace. We can approach God only by faith on the basis of Christ's shed blood on the cross.

Hebrews 9:22b lays it down: "Without shedding of blood is no remission."

Now I recognize there is a difference of opinion over why Cain's offering was rejected. I believe that when Cain brought his offering to God, there was not one drop of blood in it. By God's revelation, Cain and Abel knew that in order for sin to be covered, there had to be a blood sacrifice. God established it as His way, but Cain brought nothing from which you could draw blood.

Have you heard that expression, "You can't squeeze blood out of a turnip"? It has been suggested that particular expression was born at the altar when Cain presented his offering. I feel Cain was saying, "I'll do it my way," and he became the father of false religion. He built religion on human speculation, rather than divine revelation. Cain had his own man-made religion. You argue, "Well, but it was sacrificial." That's right. He had sacrificed and worked hard, but there was not a drop of blood anywhere.

Not Religion but Real Relationship

All the so-called religions of the world promulgate a system of good works to gain favor with their false gods, idols, and ultimate concerns. As he lay dying, for instance, Buddha called his disciples near and left them these parting words: "Brothers, follow the noble eight-fold path. Save yourselves." That is all religion has to offer: save yourselves. Christianity, the Way of the Lord Jesus Christ, calls: "Believe on the Lord Jesus Christ, and thou shalt be saved . . ." (Acts 16:31).

Now you can agree with the blood or you can disagree with it. But it is the true plan of God. People who have religion can sit in church every Sunday, but have no real relationship with the Lord Jesus Christ.

In Jude 11 Cain is spoken about: "Woe unto them! for they have gone in the way of Cain" (11a). The way of Cain is one of woe.

Mankind's Way Won't Make It

People with poor eyesight like "Mr. Magoo" or under nervous circumstances or not able to read have experienced tragic consequences because they *thought* they were doing right—acid in the eyes instead of eyedrops, poison instead of proper medication, an accidental overdose or underdose of medicine, severe—even fatal—accidents, and yet they thought they were doing right, using the right medication in the right dosage, walking or driving in the right direction, and the like. One can think he is right but be *deathly wrong*.

In Proverbs 14:12, the Bible says, "There is a way which seemeth right unto a man; but the end therof are the ways of death." There is only one plan of salvation, but here are the avenues of death. When a person decides "I'll do it my way," that individual may have a zeal for God but not in accordance with knowledge. For not knowing about God's righteousness and, instead, seeking to establish their own, people do not subject themselves to the righteousness of God.

The devil is lurking on every corner to convince man to worship himself rather than God. The devil is not so concerned that a person will enter the house of worship, will even walk the aisle, will be baptized, become a member of the church. But the devil is dreadfully concerned that a person will bow his head and cry, "Lord Jesus, I'm a sinner, and by your shed blood on Calvary, I come to You and trust You as my Savior."

Somewhere people have picked up the notion that they can patronize God, that they can come by occasionally and give God a little pat on the back, and say, "Lord, I'm going to be all right," when, in fact, matters are not going to be, and they know it in their hearts. They have tried to fool themselves.

Cain knew that a blood offering was required, but he chose rather to worship his own way, but Abel "brought of the firstlings of his flock." Abel believed what God taught about the shedding of blood. Abel came by faith. Now where did Abel find his faith? Where we all must get it. "Faith cometh by hearing, and hearing by the word of God" (Rom. 10:17).

God had revealed himself to Cain and Abel, and to Adam and Eve. They knew full well how they must approach God in worship. Abel worshiped God by faith and gave a blood sacrifice.

Certain skeptics have the idea that Jesus' death on the cross was an afterthought of God—that when mankind sinned, then God said, "I must think of some emergency measure to get man out of this." Don't ever believe that.

When did God have in His mind the sacrificial death of Jesus on Calvary's tree? When He flung the stars into place and when He hung this world in space. God had already devised His plan of redemption before the beginning of time. God provided for a blood sacrifice before the foundation of the world.

We must come to God by faith, or we shall not come at all. There is no other way. The writer of Hebrews speaks of the condition of worship, for he states, "By faith Abel offered unto God a more excellent sacrifice than Cain, by which he obtained witness from God that he was righteous."

If God Calls You Righteous, You Are!

My hope is built on nothing less
Than Jesus' blood and righteousness
I dare not trust the sweetest frame
But wholly lean on Jesus' Name.

On Christ the Solid Rock I stand,
All other ground is sinking sand,
All other ground is sinking sand.

—Edward Mote

If God declares us righteous through Jesus Christ, some-day all of us in Him will be in heaven.

In heaven you're going to exclaim, "Well, there's my pastor. He made it after all. Sometimes I wasn't quite sure. I mean, I wondered about him. But there he is."

And I'm going to remark, "Well, now, that looks like some of my former church members. Hmm, I guess they've changed a little bit from the way I knew them, but here they are." We might question one another's presence in heaven, and we might ask Jesus, "Lord, did you see that church member over there? Oh, Jesus, how did he make it?" Jesus is going to reply, "I don't see anything." You know why? Because their sins have been covered by the blood of the Lamb. We're going to be in heaven declared righteous. God is going to view us through the righteousness of Jesus Christ.

Hebrews 11:4 makes it plain that the condition of worship is obedience to God. If you are truly going to worship, you must do it God's way. If you are going to be saved, you must be saved God's way. You "must needs go home by the way of the cross, There's no other way but this." Abel presented a blood sacrifice, and Cain and Abel knew what God wanted. Abel offered blood. Cain did not. God's Word is explicit, "Neither is there salvation in any other: for there is none other name under heaven given among men, whereby, we must be saved" (Acts 4:12). False religion calls for another name or names. There is only one name—the blessed name of Jesus.

Have you ever noticed that the world lives by absolutes with the exception of religion and morality? We are to live by the laws of our land, and if we break those laws and standards, we must be punished. We live by absolutes in physics and biochemistry and other areas.

When you visit the doctor and you have a problem, you ordinarily want to hear the facts. Now no one likes to hear that they have been diagnosed with a terrible disease. But wouldn't you still rather know the truth than to remain ignorant about a serious illness? Then, once you have a diagnosis, you want a cure. Suppose your physician were to suggest, "You have terminal cancer, and I presently know what can be done about it—in fact, it may produce a miracle"? And he continued, "You may be able to live longer than we'd ever think, but rather than that, why don't you just go home and do whatever you think best, and we'll see what happens"? You wouldn't like that one bit. Why? Because we have come to depend on certain medical truths which we consider to be absolute, factual, and reliable. So we trust them.

God has given us absolutes and standards in religion and morality, and those outside of Christ answer, "There are a number of ways to go about this." The devil constantly works to spread this kind of tripe. The sin of mankind without salvation in Christ will concoct far-fetched notions.

The lost world claims there are no absolutes in religion, and that is exactly what many boys and girls are being taught through programs of values clarification in the schools of America. They are taught situation ethics: that is that the person becomes the absolute, and at that moment, when facing a moral, ethical conflict or dilemma, he makes the decision. He does what he feels is right.

But God has His own absolutes. "Wherewithal shall a young man cleanse his way? by taking heed thereto according to thy word. . . . Thy word is a lamp unto my feet, and a light unto my path" (Ps. 119:11,105).

God is our absolute, and He gives us absolutes by which we are to live. It is amazing that even Christians can twist moral issues out of shape? The "new age" movement, which is the "Old Age" movement that originated with Lucifer, befuddles many a Christian. Many believers do exactly what Cain was doing. They come to the house of God, but they retort, "But, God, those things in Your Holy Word are fine and good. I'm going to live by some of them, but, Lord, you know that's rather restrictive and too narrow, and I don't want to walk on the narrow way. The narrow way is as broad as Jesus, and that's as broad as a person needs to be in order to experience fulfillment and joy in his life.

It is staggering how many people will abandon their moral convictions and then somehow alibi, "Oh, but Lord, you understand my dilemma." He certainly does, and He has given us the way out in the Lord Jesus Christ, not through mankind's blundering way.

Cain refused to worship God on God's terms. So, God refused to accept his sacrifice, and the Bible records, "Cain went out from the presence of the Lord . . . (Gen. 4:16a). "Woe unto them! for they have gone in the way of Cain" (Jude 11a).

When Abel arrived to worship, it was in obedience. He brought a lamb without spot or blemish. Perhaps he built a small altar of stones and set fire to the kindling. He picked up that little lamb, and you can almost envision that little, trusting lamb. That "little lamb, whose fleece was white as snow." That lamb's big, liquid eyes gazed into the eyes of Abel. When Abel touched that little lamb, it trembled. And Abel must have thought, *How can I do it?* Then he seized the knife and slashed the throat of that lamb. As the blood spurted, the life began to flow from the lamb until finally it was a lifeless form. No doubt with deep sorrow and tears running down his cheeks, Abel lifted up that silent form—because of his own sin, he offered it to God as a sacrifice.

You may exclaim, "What a horrible way to approach God!" Oh, but sin is dreadful. We'll almost shed a tear over the death of that precious lamb, but then we may overlook the precious Lamb of God who sat in the Garden of Gethsemane and wept, "Not My will, but Thine be done."

Our hearts should be aflame for what God has done for us. We should hardly think of the shed blood of Jesus as He died on the cross without shedding a tear, and thus seeing our sin.

The first sacrifice was Abel's lamb—one lamb for one person. Later came the Passover—one lamb for one family. Then arrived the Day of Atonement (Yom Kippur) when the high priest would enter the Holy of Holies, and there would be one lamb sacrificed for one nation. Finally there was Good Friday, and it was one Lamb for the whole world! John the Baptist shouted, "Behold the Lamb of God, which taketh away the sin of the world" (John 1:29).

Abel, and everyone else with saving faith, had his faith counted for righteousness. Without the shedding of blood there is no forgiveness. By faith, Abel looked through the telescope of faith all the way to the cross.

Once I received a phone call from a woman who was seriously troubled and in tears. She explained, "I had a terrible dream last night, and this morning I read the Bible. As I read it, I became more desperate, because I came to verses of Scripture I didn't understand." And she asked, "Would you interpret Hebrews 10:26 for me?" I opened my Bible and read, "For if we sin willfully after that we have received the knowledge of the truth, there remaineth no more sacrifice for sins." And she sobbed, "Oh, Pastor, is there any way for me to be forgiven of my sin, or does that mean there is no forgiveness?"

That Scripture, I pointed out, describes a person who knows the truth but rejects Christ's sacrifice, just as Cain rejected the sacrifice which God demanded. And when people reject Christ's way, there is no other acceptable sacrifice for sin. With delight I told her, "Yes, God will forgive you of your sin. You come to Him by faith."

Joyfully she replied, "Well, I've made a decision. When I was twelve years old and I walked the aisle with a group of other kids, I wasn't saved." Then she prayed over the phone to receive Jesus Christ as her Savior.

All of those years she had been trying to be saved Cain's way. She had tried to pray night after night to be saved, but it had not worked. She finally came to realize Jesus would flood her soul once and for all if she would come to Him by faith. Then the Lamb of God would take away the sin in her life by His shed blood on Calvary.

The biblical principle prevails, "The wages of sin is death; but the gift of God is eternal life through Jesus Christ our Lord" (Rom. 6:23). God took our place, all our sin, all our shame, and all our blame. He, who knew no sin, died for us.

Have you ever, burdened in your sin, come to God and cried, "Lord, in my hand no price I bring, simply to Thy cross I cling"?

Think of it. When you sin, there's nothing you can bring— none of your goodness, only your unworthiness. You cannot come to Jesus bringing an offering of the "best you can do." All you can do is come and trust in the shed blood of Jesus Christ and confess, "Lord, I have nothing."

The Lamb of God bowed His head on the cross and called out, "It is finished." The price was paid in full. In the dawn of civilization, with Abel and Cain, God was trying to teach us: "Without shedding of blood is no remission." The red river of Jesus' blood flows out of the Garden of Eden and for all time until Jesus comes again. Our sins must be covered by His blood.

Maybe you reply, "I don't believe it. I just don't agree." God's Word has a definitive word for you, "The preaching of the cross is to them that perish foolishness; but unto us which are saved it is the power of God" (1 Cor. 1:18). "I must needs go home by the way of the cross, There's no other way but this. I shall ne'er get sight of the gates of light. If the way of the cross I miss."

Cain became so angry that God would not accept him, in his own man-made worship, that Cain killed his brother Abel. His other distinction is that he was the first murderer in history.

James aptly wrote, "Then when lust hath conceived, it bringeth forth sin: and sin, when it is finished, bringeth forth death" (1:15). It will happen every time. You might comment, "Well, I'm still alive." Sin, when it is finished, brings forth death.

There are only two ways of worship. One leads to hell, the other, to heaven. One is the way of Cain, but "Woe unto them that would follow in the way of Cain." The other is the way of Abel, the way of the cross. Which way are you following?

John Newton, "a wild beast tamed by Jesus," wrote in his hymn-poem, "In Evil Long I Took Delight":

> Thus, while His death my sin displays
> In all its blackest hue,
> Such is the mystery of grace,
> It seals my pardon too.
> With pleasing grief, and mournful joy,
> My spirit now is fill'd,
> That I should such a life destroy,—
> Yet live by Him I kill'd!

Note

1. John Phillips, *Exploring Hebrews* (Chicago: Moody Press, 1977), 162.

2.

Walking with God

Hebrews 11:5; Genesis 5:24; Jude 14-15

By faith Enoch was translated that he should not see death: and was not found, because God had translated him: for before his translation he had this testimony, that he pleased God. Hebrews 11:5

As we study "God's Hall of Faith," we focus on Enoch. "By faith Enoch was translated that he should not see death; and was not found, because God had translated him; for before his translation he had this testimony, that he pleased God. But without faith it is impossible to please him: for he that cometh to God must believe that he is, and that he is a rewarder of them that diligently seek him" (Heb. 11:5-6).

Now here was a man who pleased God. Why and how did he please God? Because he walked by faith. In fact, there is no other way to please God.

"But without faith it is impossible to please him." Now do you believe God's Word? Outside of faith there is no way to please God.

Now Enoch pleased God to the extent that one day God and he took a walk, and they decided to keep on walking. They walked until they entered into heaven.

Enoch lived midway between the fall in the Garden of Eden and the flood of the earth. Many do not realize it, but Adam was still living when Enoch was born! Adam was 622 years old when Enoch was born. Now you may inquire, "Do you really believe that men lived that long in those days?" Yes, I do. Well, then, do you know why they were able to live that long? It was because sin had yet not taken its toll. Sin had already caused people's bodies to deteriorate. What we are facing today—the farther we are from the Garden of Eden, when God made man in His own image and gave him paradise, and then man fell—is the reality of the fact that the longer we live the more we have to cope with the consequences of our sin. So when Enoch was born, Adam was 622 years old. You might say he was just in "the prime of life." Adam lived 308 years of the 376 which Enoch lived on earth. The Bible records that Adam lived to be 930 years old, and he was only at midlife when Enoch was born.

When Enoch was born, his father Jared was 162 years old. Why, when you hear that, you comment that he must have married awfully young, to have a child that young—162 years old! Jared lived 962 years. That means he lived only seven years less than the oldest man who ever lived on this earth. Good old Methuselah!

They Sure Lived a Long Time!

Jared lived 962 years of age, and he was Enoch's father. Methuselah lived 969, and he was Enoch's son. Enoch lived 376 years on earth and kept right on living. He never died!

In chapter 5 of Genesis, we read about the generations of Adam. There we learn the story of Enoch, and you will also discover in that chapter, there is the little phrase, "and he died," eight times. "And he died," "and he died." It is like walking through a cemetery and reading the headstones. But when you reach Enoch, the Bible makes the succinct statement, "And Enoch walked with God: and he was not; for God took him."

Enoch was the only man in that chapter about whom it does not record, "And he died." Why? Because Enoch was translated into heaven. He did not taste of death. There is a little riddle that goes like this. "The oldest man who ever lived, who died before his daddy did, who was that?" He was Methuselah, the oldest man who ever lived. He died before his daddy did because his daddy, Enoch, never died.

In Hebrews 11:5-6 there is a *warning* from God, a *word* of God, and a *walk* with God.

"But without faith it is impossible to please God." Have

you ever thought about that name Methuselah? Can you imagine Enoch and his wife sitting around discussing what they were going to name their newborn. And they decided, "If he's a boy, we're going to name him Methuselah." That is not the average, spur-of-the-moment name. Then, what does Methuselah mean? It means, "It shall be sent when he is dead." Or, "when he is gone, it will come." Now what was God revealing to Enoch in the naming of his boy? God was indicating, "When this boy dies, the judgment will be coming."

What happened? Remember that the judgment was coming. "When he is gone, it shall come." Strange. The judgment is coming. Now listen to this. The very year that Methuselah died, the windows of heaven opened. The rains descended, and the flood came—yes, that same flood that destroyed all the living creatures of the earth, except those who had boarded Noah's boat. So, in naming his son Methuselah, Enoch received a warning from God that God's "spirit shall not always strive with man" (Gen. 6:3).

You might remark, "But look how long Methuselah lived!" Look how long it was before the judgment came. Yes, but Peter wrote, "God is long-suffering to us-ward, not willing that any should perish, but that all should come to repentance" (2 Pet. 3:9b).

God is infinitely patient. But write it down: the judgment of God is not always swift, but it is always sure.

God Is Patient, but . . .

Years ago out West a farmer who claimed to be an atheist wrote a letter to the editor of a local newspaper: "Sir, I have been trying an experiment with a field of mine. I plowed it on Sunday. I planted it on Sunday. I cultivated it on Sunday. I reaped it on Sunday. I hauled it into my barn on Sunday. And now, Mr. Editor, what is the result? I have more bushels to the acre from that field than any of my neighbors have had this October." He was taken aback by the editor's reply (and the editor himself was not especially religious). Underneath the letter the editor published this comment: "God does not always settle His accounts in October."

God warned Enoch, and Enoch warned the people of his day. In fact, jot down Jude 14-15. Those verses speak about Enoch prophesying to the people about their wickedness and worldliness, and how they were going to be judged by the righteousness of God. There were many wicked, rough-hewn people living in Enoch's day. He preached to a generation that did not want to hear that judgment was coming. Prophetic preaching is not popular today, either. The preachers of the Word of God today preach to this generation a judgment of fire. As surely as the old world was destroyed by the flood, this present world is going to be destroyed by fire.

God revealed to Enoch that He couldn't let the people continue to live in their wickedness and open rebellion against Almighty God. That day is coming for us. God is going to cry, "That's enough. I can't take it anymore. Now is the time for Me to move in judgment. I can't let them live anymore." Jesus preached, "But as the days of Noah were, so shall also the coming of the Son of man be" (Matt. 24:37). When Jesus comes, this wayward world is going to be judged. The Bible states, "Enoch walked by faith, and he warned the people that without faith it is impossible to approach God." How did Enoch possibly know that? Because God revealed His prophecy to Enoch in the naming of his son "Methuselah." "When he is gone, it shall come." Oh, what are we to do? We sing B. B. McKinney's song so well. "Have faith in God, He's on His throne. Have faith in God. He watches o'er His own. He cannot fail. He must prevail. Have faith in God. Have faith in God."

There is not only a warning from God. There is the *word of God*. This passages goes, "By faith Enoch was translated," and then notice in verse 6, "for he that cometh to God must believe." You may hear God's warning in your heart. You may sense fear, but fear is not enough. If fear is all you feel about the coming of Jesus, all you have about the destruction of this world someday, all you have about the judgment of God, then you do not have enough. "You must have faith." Enoch walked by faith.

Now neither you nor I have ever had faith apart from the revelation of God. When the Bible uses terms like "by faith" and "must believe," we are made aware that Enoch had received a word from God.

In Romans 10:17 there is the principle, "Faith cometh by hearing and hearing" by what? By "the word of God." Now make a note: faith is simply believing what God says. His Word is the word of faith. Without faith it is impossible to please God. Enoch's first action was to decide to walk by faith, to take God at His Word, to agree with Him. That is faith.

You Have to Walk "in Sync"

Amos the prophet rhetorically asked, "Can two walk together, except they be agreed?" (Amos 3:3). Of course, the answer is no. Two people cannot walk together in intimate fellowship unless they are agreed. Marriages are flying apart today because there is no agreement between husbands and wives; and when there is no agreement, there will be no intimacy and no fellowship. When two people cannot agree, then they cannot really walk together. Enoch *walked with God*, so obviously he was in agreement with Him.

But Enoch did pass through a time of rebellion. He lived sixty-five years outside the faith. The Bible notes in Genesis that "Enoch walked with God after [*after*] he begat Methuselah..." (5:22a). Enoch was sixty-five years old when Methuselah was born, but the Bible says in Hebrews 11:5, "Enoch pleased God." He pleased God through walking by faith. Want to please God? Walk by faith. In 2 Corinthians 5:7, the Bible makes it clear, "(For we walk by faith, not by sight:)." One of the difficulties with us is that we talk about faith. We know that word faith well. We have heard it all of our lives, but do we actually understand faith? If we do, do we walk by faith? What do most of us do? For we walk *by sight and not by faith.* Most of us in our Christian experience unfortunately respond to God on the basis of what we can see and what we can rationalize.

Faith is looking at that which is unseen, the invisible, seeing the unseen with our spiritual eyes, and then acting upon the unseen. Mary Irwin wrote a book entitled *Seeing the Invisible.* We are to act upon the things we see in the future, as if they were already occurring today. What we are doing is: we are claiming by faith what we ascertain through the revelation of God in His Word to be truth, as we respond by faith. We must be sure that we are walking by faith and not simply by sight.

Enoch never saw God with his naked eyes, but he believed God and walked with Him for 300 years. He just believed God was there. The Bible teaches, in essence, that faith is impossible without a willingness to believe. You can have faith only if you are willing to surrender your will to His will. Many people snarl, "Well, I'm going to do it my way. I'm going to come to God however I want to." So they never come to God because faith is the way, and without faith it is impossible to approach God.

The surrender of your will must be totally willing. The surrender must be unconditional. The surrender of Japan and Germany was called "unconditional"—absolute, complete, total, unqualified. You must surrender to God in love by faith. People often come to God with a spirit of resignation, saying, "I've just tried everything else, and I know God's up there somewhere. Since I've tried everything else, and it hasn't worked, then I'm just going to resign myself to doing it God's way." But that is not genuine faith. Faith is a willing surrender. Faith is praying, "Lord, I want to surrender to Your will." When we genuinely come to God, we do it gladly and with a full, free "laying down of arms." He is not going to force us into commitment. Come to Him by faith.

God gave Enoch a *warning*, and God gave Enoch His *word*. "Enoch walked with God."

Genesis 5:24 corresponds to Hebrews 11:5. "And Enoch walked with God: and he was not; for God took him" (v. 24). And Enoch walked with God. Now what does that mean? It indicates that he walked and walked and walked. I think he was athletic; I feel his heartbeat was exactly right—because he walked and walked and walked, and that wasn't all. His spiritual heartbeat was just right because he kept on walking with God.

You may be in the best physical shape in the world, but your heartbeat is not right until you are walking with God. He walked for three centuries, until he walked right into heaven.

In the Greek of Hebrews 11:5, the word "translated" is *metatithemi*. I dearly love the sound of that word, but what does it mean? It is derived from two Greek words, *meta* (meaning "with") and *tithemi* which means "to replace, to exchange, to transfer, to carry over." The word means that Enoch was transposed or carried over. When he was translated, he simply exchanged a place on earth for one in heaven. God loved him so much, he beckoned, "Enoch, come on. We're going home to glory." Enoch did not die; he merely changed places.

Hebrews 11:6 speaks of God as a rewarder of them that diligently seek him." The Bible says, "And you will seek me, and find me when you search for me with all your heart." When we walk with God, we walk in a fellowship, a shared life, "simpatico," to use a good Hispanic word. In Galatians 5:16 we read, "walk in the Spirit, and ye shall not fulfill the lust of the flesh." Do you believe that? Do you believe the Bible? Do you accept Galatians 5:16 by faith? Do you honestly believe that God will give you victory over sin and the temptation to sin? Do you believe that God will see you through? If you do, you must accept that and every other word from God by faith. Our walk with God is a walk of fellowship, and walking with God is pleasing to Him. Maybe Enoch was breaking out in song. We should sing, "He walks with me, and He talks with me, and He tells me I am His own." Every believer must walk every day with God on this earth—and when we reach heaven, we'll walk with Him forever.

It is impossible for an unbeliever to have a walk with God, impossible for an unbeliever to have fellowship with Him (see 2 Cor. 6:14-16). Why? Because the natures are too different between God and man.

Walking Right into Heaven

When we walk with the Lord in the light of His Word
What a glory He sheds on our way!
....
While we do His good will He abides with us still,
And with all who will trust and obey,

....
Then in fellowship sweet we will sit at His feet
Or we'll walk by His side in the way.
—John S. Sammis

What a fellowship as we walk with Him, later to "step from this earth to God's heaven so fair."

Let me give you an example. You can take your dog for a walk, but you cannot walk with your dog. Your dog can provide you companionship but cannot provide you fellowship. When we walk with the Lord, it is a time of fellowship.

When Enoch was translated, "he was not." It teaches us that the people of the world missed Enoch when he disappeared. They probably thought he died. Isn't that how people are? When you live for God, detractors will say, "His standards are too rigid, his beliefs are too old-fashioned, and his example is too narrow." But once he is gone, he is missed by saint and sinner alike. They no doubt tried to find Enoch, but they couldn't. He had gone to glory. The world does not understand that we the children of God are preserving this chaotic world while we are here. Neither does it understand the part the Christian plays in this world. The Christian, by the Spirit of God, brings order to this world. That often allows the unbeliever to go fairly well about doing what he wants to do, "his own thing." And when we are raptured, this world is going to fall into chaos and disorder because the Spirit of God will exit with us. The Spirit of God lives in our hearts today by the transformation of God in our lives as we trust Jesus as our personal Savior.

Enoch's being translated into heaven is a picture of what is going to happen to us someday if we are living when Jesus comes. We will be translated into heaven (see 1 Thess. 3:13-18). We call it the rapture, being caught up to meet Him in the clouds. When Jesus comes all of those who are walking with God on this earth will meet the Lord in the air—when the trumpet blows, when the angel shouts. Like Enoch, we will be translated to be with Him.

You ask, "what should we do?" We ought to live here in such a fashion that when we are gone, people will miss us. We ought to live in a Christ-like manner. We ought to live a godly life as we walk with God. "And Enoch walked with God." Do you?

According to Solomon there is nothing new under the sun, but this bears repeating. An elderly Christian gentleman was anticipating being with Jesus. He shouted, "I'm not looking for the undertaker. I'm looking for the Uppertaker!" Are you looking for Him?

3.

Rising Above the Flood

Hebrews 11:7; Genesis 6:1-16

By faith Noah, being warned of God of things not seen as yet, moved with fear, prepared an ark to the saving of his house; by the which he condemned the world, and became heir of the righteousness which is by faith. Hebrews 11:7

"By faith Noah, being warned of God of things not seen as yet, moved with fear, prepared an ark to the saving of his house; by the which he condemned the world, and became heir of the righteousness which is by faith" (Heb. 11:7).

Noah was called "a preacher of righteousness." Noah had a close communion with God. "Noah was a righteous man, blameless in his time; Noah walked with God" (Gen. 6:9). He was a man not perfect, a sinner as we are sinners. Nevertheless, he was blameless before God, because by faith he had embraced God; he knew the forgiveness of sin and was seen as righteous by God. That is, God had declared him righteous by his faith. He was "justified" by faith, and the Lord looked on him as though he had never sinned.

Faith is a series of steps. We first are to worship God by faith. Salvation is through faith. We are justified by faith; there is no other way to be saved than by faith. God has promised if we will receive Christ as Savior, we will have heaven for all eternity. We will sit and stand before the throne of God. This is not the end, but in Christ there is a beginning that never ends!

The Cross and Noah's Ark

"There is a tradition that has come down through the centuries that the one and only door of Noah's ark was shaped like a cross, and thus typified that heaven and salvation are arrived at only through the cross of Christ. There

41

may be no foundation for this tradition, but we do know that
Christ is the only door to heaven. If we ever arrive at the
destination we do it through Him who is our Lord and
Savior."[1]

Until we are in heaven the abiding presence of the Holy
Spirit resides in our hearts. We are saved as we respond to
God in faith—by His grace, not our goodness. We learn to
worship God. When a person is saved, he/she wants to
worship God. He wants to be at the house of God with the
people of God. He wants praise to God, "Thank you for
saving my soul."

I have never understood the person who wanted to argue
that one does not have to attend church to be saved. Yes, that
person's point is right. One can be saved anywhere he bows
his head and prays to receive Christ, asking forgiveness for
his sins. You can worship whenever you tune your heart
toward God. The moment you turn your face toward God to
worship Him, you are standing on holy ground. The person
who is saved will long for praise and worship. One difficulty
with thousands of church members is that they stay away
from the house of God.

Yet, it is possible for a person to be carnal and yet be saved.
But the carnal person has every reason to be worried that
perhaps he does not know the Lord Jesus Christ as Savior.
When the Spirit of God is in a person, He changes his life,
and he wants to worship God. From the beginning of time,
God has taught us to worship Him. We are to worship the
Lord in the beauty of holiness. How I love songs of praise,
along with the traditional hymns, which have blessed us.
Many people attend church and yet have never learned how
to worship. They are so restricted and so bound, perhaps by
tradition or by personal opinion. As we worship Him, there
is a sense of freedom in the Lord Jesus. Let us praise the
Lord and have joy in our hearts and happiness upon our
faces—to let the world know that Jesus saves.

Abel teaches us about *worship* by faith. In the life of Enoch, we are aware of a *walk* with God. And Enoch was translated into heaven. And we come so we are to walk with Him, day in and day out, every hour, every moment, and every second. Our life with God is progressive. First we worship the Lord. Then as we begin worshiping Him, we walk with Him. Then we begin to understand what it is to *work* by faith. When we worship by faith and when we walk by faith, then we will begin to work by faith.

Paul wrote in Ephesians 2:10, we are "created in Christ Jesus, unto good works which God before has ordained that we should walk in them." We are not saved by works but by the glorious grace of God and our faith in the Lord Jesus Christ. We are not saved by works, but we are saved *by a faith that works*. In Hebrews 11, you will recognize that faith was demonstrated by these men through what they did.

Noah's Faith and the Coming Deluge

In Noah we have faith triumphing over judgment. Here again we are called to contemplate a man who in a dark and difficult day heard the voice of God in his inmost soul, and was oracularly warned of Him concerning something which, in the very nature of things, he could not see; but he believed God and, moved with fear, prepared an ark for the saving of his house. By acting thus upon the Word of the Lord, he condemned the world and became heir of the righteousness which is according to faith. The very building of the ark was in itself a sermon to the antediluvians. Every tap of Noah's hammer was a part of his preaching of righteousness to that generation. It declared him to be a man of faith, and it manifested their utter unbelief.[2]

Noah *lived* by faith. That means he lived in total obedience to God. When God spoke that was all Noah needed. How is it with you? When God says it, you should say, "That settles it, and I'll do it, Lord." When God says it, do you go to your best friend and explain, "I have the strangest impression. I just don't know what to do with it. Why, let me tell you what it is, and see what you think"? Then you fill them in, and they are astounded by it. That friend may reply, "Don't bother about that. Why, if you just won't do anything about it, it'll go away." Friendly counsel is OK, but what God wants counts.

There are four aspects we discover in Hebrews 11:7, about the life of Noah, and thus about the life-style of a man or woman of faith.

In this verse there are four facts: a word, a work, a world, and a worth. Noah first of all listened to a *word* of fate. "By faith Noah, being warned of God of things not seen as yet, moved with fear. . . . Now that word fear literally indicates reverence. It does not mean to be afraid. Noah was not afraid of the Word of God in his life. He was reverencing God as he had a sense of holy awe before the Almighty. He was moved by the fact that he was in the presence of God. What was God's warning?

Now we turn to the warning God gave. "And the Lord said, My spirit shall not always strive with man, for that he also is flesh; yet his days shall be an hundred and twenty years" (Gen. 6:3). God was preparing to judge the people of Noah's day. Even God was fed up with that wicked generation. How do you think He feels about today? God allotted 120 years for them to repent of their sins.

Now you may think, *Man, if I had 120 years, I'd be dead before that.* But remember in that generation, soon after the paradise of Eden, sin had not yet polluted the world to the extent that the lives of people were shortened like ours. Men were living 600, 700, 800, and 900 years.

God's Spirit Shall Not Always Strive with Man

What a surprise was in the offing!

"My spirit shall not always strive with man," God warned. "And God looked upon the earth, and, behold, it was corrupt." Then He lowered the boom, "The end of all flesh is come before me; for the earth is filled with violence through them; and, behold, I will destroy them with the earth . . ." (Gen. 6:12-13). Then he prophesied the coming of the flood.

In Hebrews 11:7 Noah was warned by God "of things not seen as yet." What were those things Noah had not seen? Noah had never seen rain, and if Noah had never seen rain, Noah had never beheld a flood. And yet God prophesied, "I am going to destroy the earth by a flood."

In Noah's day, it had never rained before. You ask, "How do you know that?" Look at Genesis 2:6, "But there went up a mist from the earth and watered the whole face of the ground." The earth was watered in those early days by a mist which came up through the ground. It also appears that there was a mist in the atmosphere surrounding the earth (Gen. 1:7). It never had rained before, and yet God was prophesying a flood. Can you understand how difficult it was to have faith in that day, when God warned, "I am going to send a flood," and people would exclaim, "A flood, a flood. What's a flood? A flood, there has never been a drop of rain on this earth. How could there be a flood?"

Noah was moved to reverence at the warning of God. Because he reverenced God he worshiped God and took God at His word, at face value. He did what God told him to do. Noah was a man of obedient faith who listened to the voice of the Lord.

Then there was a *work* of faith. Noah "prepared an ark to the saving of his house." When God spoke, Noah dropped everything he was doing and started building an ark. That's faith to the nth degree!

Can you imagine the Bible records that God instructed Noah to build an ark out of gopher wood? Most scholars believe that the gopher is a type of cypress wood, and cypress wood does not rot easily. One of the greatest acts of faith in all of history was Noah picking up an ax and beginning to chop down a gopher tree. An ark was a coffin-shaped box, for instance, the Ark of the Covenant. What an unusual boat it would be—no rudder, nothing with which to steer, none of the equipment we would have on the sailboat of today. Yet the ark was being prepared to float, as per God's instructions. So Noah, faithful and dependable Noah, was building a huge ship on dry land, in an area where there were no large lakes, much less an ocean!

That would be like building an ark in Wichita Falls, Texas, or in the Kalahari Desert. If you started building a monstrous ship tomorrow, a few folks might think you're crazy. When Noah and his boys began building that ark, no one else had the faith to help with it. People would come by and inquire, "Noah what're you doing?"

And Noah would reply, "I'm building an ark."

And they would ask, "How big is your ark gonna be?"

"Well, it's gonna be about 450 feet long" [about one and one-half football fields]. He gave the specs, about seventy-three feet high and forty-two or forty-four feet wide. Then they were really intrigued. "C'mon, why are you building it?

Noah answered, "Well, God is going to send a flood."

A flood! They laughed and ridiculed old Noah. Regardless, Noah labored in faith for 120 years without doubting the word of God in his heart. God commanded him, and that was good enough for the old man. He worked twelve decades in the faith that what God prophesied was going to come true. Don't you think when it reached about ninety years, we might grow a little discouraged?

You Think Job Was Patient—What About Noah?

Noah is an indictment of our "quickie" mentality. In this frenetic age we want everything *yesterday*. Many professing Christians want to demand easy, immediate answers from the God of glory. They pray for what they want. If the *yes* does not come posthaste, they quit praying at all. A solid hour of concentrated prayer would almost kill today's quickie Christian. Noah spent 120 years building and preparing. There is no indication that he ever complained or questioned God.

God had not sent His judgment. The deluge had not arrived. Most of us would complain, "God's not come. I'm through with this faith business."

First Peter 3:20: "the long-suffering of God waited in the days of Noah, while the ark was a preparing, . . ." Why did God wait 120 years? That's a legitimate question. God waited 120 years for the same reason that the Lord Jesus Christ has already tarried 2,000 years, and He has not yet come again. He is giving every person an opportunity to trust Christ as Savior. God delays the hour, as He did in the generation of Noah. For twelve decades they continued to shake their fists in the face of God. Their response was, "It has never rained a drop in the history of this world." All the while Noah worked, he warned the people and witnessed to the people. In fact, 2 Peter 2:5 calls him "a preacher of righteousness." Finally the ark was constructed. The judgment was coming every time his crew swung a hammer, every time they sawed a plank. The hammering became a litany of condemnation and judgment: "The judgment is coming, the judgment is coming. Repent, repent."

Through the centuries skeptics have scoffed: "Where is the promise of his coming? for since the fathers fell asleep, and all things continue as they were from the beginning of the creation. For this they willingly are ignorant of, that by the word of God the heavens were of old, and the earth standing out of the water and in the water: Whereby the world that then was, being overflowed with water, perished: But the heavens and the earth, which are now, by the same word are kept in store, reserved unto fire against the day of judgment and perdition of ungodly men" (1 Pet. 3:4-7). This is how many treat the second coming of the Lord Jesus, even though the Bible teaches His imminent return. We have heard the message so long. We say, "He's not come, so surely He's not coming today." Rest assured, He is coming back.

Finally the heavens were opened, and the flooding began. Noah's ark had become commonplace; his preaching had fallen on deaf ears. Only eight people, Noah's family, entered the ark. Can you imagine preaching that long and having only eight converts? Noah was one of them, and that left his wife, his three sons, and their wives. Noah never had given up. Oh, he too had the opportunity to procrastinate. He could have alibied, "I'll just get around to it in the 100th year," but he determined he was going to walk by faith and not doubt God.

Don't Magnify Your Doubts

Mary Gardner Brainard summed it up well:

> So, I go on not knowing,
> —I would not if I might—
> I would rather walk in the dark with God
> Than go alone in the light;
> I would rather walk with Him by faith
> Than walk alone by sight.

People often remark, "Oh, doubting God is merely a part of our spiritual experience." I do not believe that. We can be bombarded with doubt. The devil will do all he possibly can to make us doubt our salvation and the will of God in our lives. Yes, doubt may pass through our minds, but a biblical faith dispels doubt. How do you rid yourself of doubt? Must you have a nervous collapse and then determine whether you are rid of your doubt? Doubt is dissolved by faith (see Dan. 5:12). Faith is believing God for what He says and then acting on it as if it has all ready occurred. That is also exactly what salvation is. You have believed what God has said in His Word, that if you trust Him, and ask forgiveness of sins, you will be saved. And so by faith you respond—you act upon it and it becomes a fact. God has never broken a promise, and that is His promise if you respond.

Noah lived by faith and worked by faith. He never doubted God. If there is doubt in your life, God can expel it (Paren-thetically, if today you are not sure of your salvation, although you may have made an attempt at a decision in earlier life, you can know. In your heart, pray, "Dear Lord Jesus, I don't know that I'm saved, and if I'm not I come to you this moment to ask forgiveness of sin and to receive You as my Savior. If you mean that with all of your heart, you will have assurance as Jesus floods your soul with His Spirit.)

Noah lived in a world of wickedness and foolishness. Hebrews 11:7c says, "By the which he condemned the world."

In Genesis 6, the Bible declares, "And God saw that the wickedness of man was great in the earth, and that every imagination of the thoughts of his heart was only evil continually" (v. 5). That sounds exactly like today. God's heart was grieved (see v. 6). In verses 6 and 7, there is the statement that "it repented the Lord" that he had made mankind.

Focus on that word "repented." In 1 Samuel 15:29, the Word states that the Lord is not a man that he should repent. So God does not repent. But here God is seen as repenting. Is there a contradiction? No! Because that word is better translated "feeling sorry for." The Lord was sorry He made man.

The Hebrew word translated "repented" literally means a sigh or an expression of regret. It implies that God's heart was broken that he had created humans. He made us to live in paradise and perfection. Since Eden we have been sinful. We are living in a world of wickedness, of vice, of immorality, of perversion which mankind has concocted. God's heart was crushed. Sin grieves God's heart when he looks upon our sin. He loves the sinner, but His wrath still falls.

Noah's Generation Sounds Like Ours

Alexander Pope's poem surely speaks of our generation and Noah's:

> Vice is a monster of so frightful mien,
> As to be hated needs but to be seen;
> Yet seen too oft, familiar with her face,
> We first endure, then pity, then embrace.

In Genesis 6:4, it says that these men of Noah's day were "men of renown." But they were renowned for what? For their sin! And the word "imagination" (v. 5) indicates that they were trying "to shape things as a potter" would mold his clay. Even as today wicked philosophers were trying to reshape and remold the society. Nothing has changed. They wanted people to believe what was good was bad, and what was bad was good. But if you stay with God's Word, you will remain on course. I am not referring to a religious experience, going to church, or simply doing good. Latch onto the Word of God, open it, proclaim it, live it, stand by it, and set it as your standard, your norm. Before long, you will be running counter even to some of the people who are closest to you. This world does not accept the Word of God as an absolute, but that was the very secret of Noah's life of faith. He heard a word from God and obeyed. The question is: am I willing to study the Word of God and accept it as the Word of God to my heart? Once I have studied it, am I willing to obey His word?

"But as in the days of Noah were, so shall also the coming of the Son of man be. For in the days that were before the flood they were eating and drinking, marrying and giving in marriage, until the day Noah entered into the ark" (Matt. 24:37-38). When the rains began in Noah's day people were eating and drinking and marrying and giving in marriage. In spite of Noah's prolonged preaching, they merely yawned in the face of God. Nothing seemed to shake or stir them. They thought: "Just as certain as yesterday and today came, tomorrow will come."

James teaches that life is "but a vapor." It is here today and gone tomorrow.

Noah stood with the Word of God, even though he was mocked and ridiculed. He was a laughingstock. How strong would our lives for Christ be if, in fact, most of the people in the world were laughing at us? Move outside of your tight-knit circle, take a stand for Christ, and see what happens.

Start building your ark by faith, and the world will try to hurt you.

Hebrews 11 speaks of an individual's *worth* through the forgiveness of God as we respond by faith, and Noah "became heir of the righteousness which is by faith." Just as Noah found safety in the ark, we find our salvation in the Lord Jesus Christ. God instructed Noah, "Rooms shalt thou make in the ark" (see Gen. 6:14). That was like God speaking to this generation, "There is room at the cross for you." "In my Father's house are many mansions," Jesus explained. There is room for all who will receive Jesus as Savior and Lord.

In Genesis 6:14 there is the instruction "to pitch it within and without with pitch." Pitch was a sticky, tarry-like substance like asphalt to caulk the seam of a wooden boat inside and out, thus keeping the water out. In the Hebrew the word for "pitch" has the same root as the word for "atonement," kopher. The word pitch is the same word as atonement. What an intriguing likeness. God was telling Noah, "I want you to put the atonement on the inside and the outside so the waters of judgment cannot come in." The building of and the safety of the ark are powerful prophecies of the blood atonement of the Lord Jesus Christ. The Bible says, "Without the shedding of blood there is no remission" (Heb. 9:22). The words atonement and pitch literally mean "to cover." The blood of Jesus covers our sin.

The Flood—Judgment and Atonement

Now what did the flood represent? The judgment of God. When, then, is the atonement? It was to keep out the waters of judgment. Noah and his family were safe inside, and there was not one drop of judgment coming through.

A Sunday School teacher asked a little girl if there was anything that God cannot do. She replied, "Yes, there is one thing that God can't do. He can't see my sin through the blood of Jesus Christ!" What an understanding of the blood atonement. God has accomplished atonement for us. "The

Lord said unto Noah, Come thou and all thy house into the ark" (Gen. 7:1a). That was God's invitation as the flood was coming. The ark was prepared, but Noah still had a decision to make. Will we enter the ark or not? After all, he still had not seen a flood. Was he going to trust God to enter that ship? He exercised an act of faith. He believed God and acted on it. Faith is not simply going to work for God in the church or the community.

Many people stay busy in "religious" activities that are devoid of faith—because they have not first determined the Word of God and believed God for that Word. Can you imagine Noah's excitement as he launched out on faith? No doubt he was singing in his soul. His wife and his three sons and their wives entered the ark with Noah. They had been a puny minority on this earth.

Did you ever think about that? Noah and his folks went into the ark in the minority and came out of the ark in the majority. He was with God. God plus nothing is a majority. The judgment of God is real and sure. The judgment of God is coming again, even with the patience of our Lord. Do you walk by faith? Do you live by faith? The Bible states that when Noah and his family entered the ark, "the Lord shut him in" (Gen. 6:16). The Lord shut Himself up inside the ark with Noah and his family and left the rest of the world to wrath, damnation, and destruction. The Lord was right there in the ark. We have to make sure that *we* are in the ark through the blood of Jesus Christ, that our sins are under the blood, and that we are covered and sealed by the Lord. God had control of the door, and Noah had charge of the window. God shut the door, and Noah had no control over it, but Noah did control the window. And God said, "Make that window above, in the top." While the flood waters were coming up, and the people all over the known world were drowning, Noah was looking out the window. Looking out the window, Noah had to look up—to see God. While all of that was happening, the eyes of Noah were fastened upon God.

In faith, the Bible says, "set your affection on things above." Put your life on the gangplank of faith and look up to God. That includes you and me. Have faith in God.

> Have faith in God, He's on His throne,
> Have faith in God, He watches o'er His own;
> He cannot fail, He must prevail;
> Have faith in God, have faith in God.
> —B. B. McKinney

Notes

1. Paul E. Holdcraft, Compiler, *Cyclopedia of Bible Illustrations* (Nashville: Abingdon Press, 1957), 90.
2. H. A. Ironside, *Studies in the Epistle to the Hebrews* (New York: Loizeaux Brothers, Inc., 1945), 135.

4.

Taking God at His Word

Hebrews 11:8; Genesis 12:1

By faith Abraham, when he was called to go out
into a place which he should after receive
for an inheritance, obeyed; and he went out, not
knowing whither he went. Hebrews 11:8

What does it mean to take God at His Word?

We speak about faith all the time, but do we truly understand it? We rave about faith, but do we live by it? We must examine ourselves to determine if we really live according to the faith we expressed as we trusted the Lord Jesus as our Savior. The Bible affirms that we are saved by God's grace and also kept by that grace. Therefore, as we are saved by our response to that grace—which is faith—then we are to live by faith.

The Proof Is in the "Faithing"

God would have us understand his way of faith. Verse 8 begins, "By faith Abraham when he was called to go out into a place which he should after receive for an inheritance, obeyed." (Abram and Abraham will often be used interchangeably, even though Abram became Abraham in Genesis 17.) Obedience is the key. We are to obey God's Word in our lives, just as Abraham obeyed as he heard the revelation of God. He obeyed. What does the Bible mean when it speaks about faith? Faith motivated all that Abraham did. By faith Abraham followed God's way and fathomed it. He came to understand that God's way is in contradiction to man's way.

You ask, "What is man's way?" Man's way says, "I won't believe it until I see it." Right? People say, "Prove it to me. I have to see it. Show me." We live in a technological, scientific age, a day of information. We have almost reached the point where if we cannot read it on a computer, it is not true. You cannot put God in a test tube, cannot break Him down into a quotient, cannot input Him into a system. Can you see what a contradiction that is? We have only two choices. Faith or lack of faith. If you are not living by faith, it means you are living by sight. Faith is our response to the revelation of God.

Five Fundamentals of Faith

There are five fundamentals of faith we can learn in verses 8-10. First, I will treat the three fundamentals of faith found in verse 8. Later, in verse 9 we will discover how Abraham lived by faith, and then verse 10 will delineate how Abraham looked by faith. One, in verse 8, we *learn by faith*. You may reply, "I didn't know that."

Two, we *leave by faith*. Absolutely, we leave by faith. There would not be a missionary in all the world if, in fact, a person did not come to the place in his life where he prayed, "Dear God, I will leave what is behind, and I will press toward the mark of what you have laid out in front of me." In fact, it is impossible for any of us to *live* by faith until we are willing to *leave* by faith.

I am not merely talking to some of you God may be calling to be missionaries. This relates to every last one of us. There is only one right manner of living, and that is to be willing to leave anything God wants you to leave, and when you leave, you are to *leave it by faith*. Then let this grab you. Abraham teaches us that we are to *leap* by faith. You come back with, "It's been a long while since I've leaped." That is simply the point I'm making. It's time to start leaping. We are to learn by faith, we are to leave by faith, we are to leap by faith, and then we are to live by faith and look by faith.

Notice that verse 8 begins with, "By faith Abraham." That is so unadorned, isn't it? At first reading you would inquire, "Is there anything really profound about that?" It teaches us that Abraham learned by faith. Abraham grew up in a pagan home with no godly heritage at all. His home, Ur of the Chaldees, was a city of moon worshipers. Once he was a pagan; then he became a believer. How, then, did he learn about God? He learned about God from the revelation of God Himself. God revealed Himself to Abraham, and Abraham responded by faith. That is, when God spoke, Abraham believed. Abraham no longer listened to the skeptics around him, but he put his trust in Jehovah as God. The only hope for this land is for our trust in God to become more than praise or words on our coinage. It must be "In God We Trust," and that must become every individual's personal testimony: "I'm coming to God by faith." We are to live by faith.

Learning and Living By Faith

"Do you say you do not live by faith? But you do. It is simply a matter of in what or whom your faith rests. A husband eats food cooked by his wife without having it tested to see if it contains poison. Why? Because he has faith in his wife she will not try to poison him. . . . Yet strangely, so many people become agnostics where God is concerned. This is but another of Satan's wiles by which he causes people to reject the salvation which a loving, faithful God so freely offers."[1]

Even in this information age, even though the computers may become bigger and bigger there is only one genuine way to learn—to learn *by faith*. Merely living a "good life" does not set us apart from the world. That is such a simple thought, but God repeatedly brings it to mind. There are many good people in the world who are unbelievers. If I were to ask, "Do you know anybody who is a 'good person,' but you're not sure they would go to heaven should they die today?" I believe that almost every believer would answer, "Yes, I know several unsaved people who are 'good' people." Being a good and decent person, a good father, a wonderful, loving husband, a sweet wife, an outstanding citizen, a successful businessman, a gracious woman does not take saving faith.

Of course, when you have faith, you want to have all of those attributes and qualities. Why? Because "God so loved *me* that He sent His only Son that *I* may have eternal life." Therefore, you pray, "Lord, I pray that I might live a life according to the teachings of Your Word so my life will honor You who has made it possible for me to know salvation."

God does indeed want us to live a good life, but that is not what makes us distinctive. What separates us from the un-saved? One word—faith. The Scriptures teach that we do not earn our relationship with the Lord Jesus. Please grasp this true principle. It is critical. To earn something and to have faith in something are mutually exclusive of each other. We do not learn by earning. We learn by faithing. Jesus invited, "Learn of me; for I am meek and lowly in heart: and ye shall find rest unto your souls" (Matt. 11:29). Do you know why there are multitudes of restless believers in this world? It is because they have failed to learn by faith. If you do not capture the reality of faith, you are failing to understand the difference between a Christian and a non-Christian. That is why the Bible teaches us it is insufficient only to live a good life. To be a true witness for the Lord Jesus is to speak His Name with our lips to another who may come under the conviction of the Holy Spirit, that they, too, may receive Christ and be saved.

Help them to recognize that the genuine good life is one lived because of one's faith in the Lord Jesus. When you learn by faith, you are going to acknowledge that you can rest in Jesus. Except by faith we cannot see with our spiritual eyes. The question arises, "Can a Christian be blinded to the truth of the Word of God, even though he knows, if he were to die now, he would go to heaven?" The answer is yes. For when we cease to grow in faith, we cannot see with spiritual eyes; thus we cannot learn God's way. Our eyes become blinded to the truth of God's Word. When that happens we are deceived into believing that we learn more by reason than we do by revelation. You really want to learn about God? You will not learn it by reason. Do you truly want to know God's will for your life? You will never really know His will by reason. Want to know God's way for your church? Not by reason. You must come to know His way by revelation.

Leaving by Faith

"I suppose that if all the times I have prayed for faith were put together, it would amount to months," commented D. L. Moody. "I used to say, 'What we want is faith; if we only have faith we can turn Chicago upside down,' or rather right side up. I thought that some day faith would come down and strike me like lightning. But faith did not seem to come. One day I read in the tenth chapter of Romans, 'Faith cometh by hearing, and hearing by the Word of God.' I had closed my Bible and prayed for faith. I now opened my Bible and began to study, and faith was been growing ever since."[2]

God expressed it, "My thoughts are not your thoughts, neither are your ways my ways, saith the Lord. For as the heavens are higher than the earth, so are my ways higher than your ways, and my thoughts than your thoughts" (Isa. 55:8-9). Oh, to learn by faith. There is no other approach for the Christian; for the non-Christian there is no other method to learn of Jesus except to receive Him—*faith*.

We are not only to learn by faith, but the text states that Abraham left by faith. So we are to leave by faith. "Abraham when he was called to go out..."! In Genesis 12 God promised Abraham, in essence, "You will do your part and I will do My part!" Are you aware that many believers have reversed that process? Insensitive believers often reach the place where they almost command, "God, *I* want to do this, and *You* make it possible!"

Do you now see what Satan would tempt us to do? Satan is a skilled deceiver. Do you apprehend why Satan would want the Christian to be blinded to the absolute, unadulterated

truth of the Word of God?—because he would be tickled for
the believer to descend to the place where he operates his life
on this twisted basis: "God, *I* will do what *I* want, and You
will help me." It was exactly the opposite with Abraham.
God ordered, "Get thee out of thy country, from thy kindred,
from thy father's house—Abraham, you do that." It was not
Abraham coming to God and reporting, "God, I think I will
do this while somewhere You can fit in." No.

God was in charge. "Abraham, you get out of the land and
away from your kinfolk. Abraham, I have a special assign-
ment for you." Then God presented him a promise after the
command. He said, "I will *show* thee. I will *make* thee a great
nation. I will *bless* thee." God gave a command and then a
promise. Why did He do it in this sequence?—because God
does not affirm us on the basis of *what we do;* God affirms us
on the basis of *what He does.*

God *told* Abraham before He *tried* Abraham. Too often a
Christian comments to himself, *I think I'll test the waters.* Soon
it is over his head. Soon he is gurgling for his last breath.
When God calls you to leave a matter behind, then you
ought to acquiesce. If God called you to leave behind material possessions, would you be willing to turn loose and do
what He wants you to do? If God asked you only to let go of
an attitude, would you? Would you surrender to let God
have His way in your life? Would you leave behind whatever
necessary that you could testify, "I'm going to live by faith.
I'm going to go with God no matter what it takes."

The Realm of the Impossible and Supernatural

Abraham had to leave his home and his Chaldean kinfolks, but listen carefully. Faith instills within us those ele-
ments which heretofore have seemed impossible to us. Once
faith sets in, even our family and our old friends never again
look the same. When you are living by faith and you are
ready to leave anything by faith, God may not call you to
leave at the moment, but you can look at your friends and

family, and you will be able to say, "If it's God's will and purpose for me to walk away from grandfathers and grandmothers and from material possessions, I could walk away from my country to go anywhere and do anything for Christ's sake." God wants not merely missionaries to respond with that determination. God wants that kind of response from all of us. God wants our willingness right at this moment. He wants us to pray, "Lord, I would be willing to leave anything which I am holding onto, and I'm willing to be detached from it for Your sake."

Abraham discovered that such was not impossible to do once he was willing to leave by faith. You may argue, "It's difficult to leave by faith!" Yes, it is, but it is not impossible. Abraham had no proof to offer another soul that he was right. He was sure of it, but he couldn't convince another person. *Naturally* we wish other people could see what we see and feel what we feel. Nevertheless, *supernaturally* we are content with the honor of God alone. When God speaks, our initial inclination is to respond by reason, but God insists that we respond to His Word by revelation.

When God commands us to "Go," we leave logic to the world, and we go with God. I love that Spanish phrase, "Vaya con Dios." "Go with God." You asked, "Chapman, are you saying to throw our minds out the window?" Well, it depends on how much we've got to throw out! No, I'm not suggesting we throw our minds out the window, but God works through your mind. Let me caution you. You are to let God speak to your mind that He might reveal Himself to your mind and your heart rather than your responding to the reasoning and standards of the world. You reach a low ebb of life when you, as a believer, live by the world's standards and according to the reason of your mind rather than the revelation of God through that mind.

Too often we forget who's leading the parade. We have no right to tell God what to do with our finite minds. God tells us what to do with His infinite mind. And there is no comparison. Oh, praise God that we have the opportunity of listening to the infinite mind of God rather than relying only on our finite minds, doing the "best we can" and wading through this world without any hope.

When God says "Go," are you ready to go? Are you willing to leave behind the baggage to which you have become attached? The first step in following God's way is the step of faith. If you will walk by faith and not by sight, God will guide you by His Word. Abraham was directed by the voice of God. God called Abraham, and Abraham followed. He began by faith to fathom God's way. So we learn by faith, leave by faith, and leap by faith. By faith Abraham left for an unknown place, unknown to him. You lament, "Poor Abraham, he had to leave it all." Oh no, faith is more than leaving— faith is leaping. Faith is not simply "from" something—faith is "to" something. Don't feel sorry for Abraham. He wasn't losing, he was gaining.

Out on the Limb for God

Helen Keller, blind and a deaf mute, was one of the rarest souls in the history of America. A devout Christian, she wrote:

> Dark as my path may seem to others, I carry a magic light in my heart. Faith, the spiritual, strong searchlight, illumines the way, and although sinister doubts lurk in the shadow, I walk unafraid toward the Enchanted Wood where foliage is always green, where joy abides, where nightingales nest and sing, and where life and death are one in the presence of the Lord.

Every time you make the leap of faith, you are gaining— not losing. The world may believe you are losing, but the Bible affirms you are gaining. You will never leap by faith until you crawl out on a limb. What is that limb? That limb is trust in God. Proverbs 3:5-6 challenges us, "Trust in the Lord with all thine heart; and lean not unto thine own understanding. In all thy ways acknowledge him and he shall direct thy paths." This world is unbearable without God. What would we do? Often when a person is hurting deeply or when people have had a death in the family, they will express exactly those words, "It would be unbearable without the Lord. Oh, what would we do without Him?" What would we do? Unfortunately and tragically we often try to run our own lives until we are slapped in the face with a crushing calamity. All too frequently we trudge along without depending on the Lord. We may have trusted in Him as our Savior, yet not be trusting in Him completely to guide us.

"Trust in the Lord with all thine heart." Jesus promised, "Come unto me . . . and I will give you rest." Trust—let that word sink in. Trust. What do you have to do when you trust? All you have to do is let go and let God have His way. When you trust, you have to trust someone, and that person should be the Lord. "Trust in the Lord with all thine heart," not merely with some of your heart, not just with a portion of your life. Trust Him. Lean on Him. Rely on Him. Count on Him. Depend on Him. He is your all in all.

He first gives us the command, exactly as He did Abraham. "Trust in the Lord . . . and he shall direct thy paths." What's wrong with the world? Well, we've messed it up. We've made everything complex when God gives us simple truths by which to live. He promises, "Trust in Me, and I will direct your paths." When we become dead to this world, we become alive unto God. Abraham had advantages but also many disadvantages. Just trust God. Does that sound simplistic? It is meant to be. Don't worry about what somebody else has. Trust God to meet the needs of your life. Rejoice in what others have. Lend a helping hand to those who have less, but for what you need, trust God. Besides considerable wealth, what did Abraham have? He had God inside him, beside him, and all around him. Abraham had all there is to have. He had faith in God and God had him.

True faith is living in this world without being of the

world. God never taught us to be isolated. When you are confronted with the cold hearts of the unredeemed, if you are not properly insulated, you are nearly going to freeze to death spiritually. If you're not insulated by the warmth of God's love and fortified by the strength of His Word, when you step out into the arctic blasts of this world without Christ, you'll be numb before you know it. You are to go into your world each day insulated by faith, but remember, *you are to go.* You are not to stay isolated from a world that is in desperate need of a Savior. When a believer in the Lord Jesus Christ fails to leap by faith day after day, he brings a coolness, and then a coldness, to the church of the living God. Why? Because he fails to insulate himself with the Word of God, the presence of God, and the power of God.

He begins to lean on his own "intuition" rather than on God's own *initiative*. When the world creeps in, coldness sets in, and a person becomes disoriented. Do you know why? Because he strays from God's way. To understand God's way means to prepare for a leap of faith. When a man is out of sync with God's way, he stumbles through this world. He will even stumble through worship stiffened by the cold winds and howling storms causing trouble with his soul. So how does the church of the Lord Jesus Christ grow cold? Through the door of one heart at a time, a heart turned cold because a person failed to insulate himself against the winter winds of the world.

Intentionally or not, it becomes winter within, and the bitter cold stiffens the supple and warm hearts which have been so open to Jesus. You ask, "How can I avoid this happening to me?" You can learn to live by faith, and you'll never learn to live by faith until you learn to leap by faith, and you'll never leap by faith until you go out on the limb of trust, and you'll never climb out on the limb of trust until you lean on Jesus and not on your own understanding. If you wait to understand why God tells you, you'll never appropriate faith. You must merely respond.

Adrian Rogers of Bellevue Baptist Church, Memphis, tells
the story of a little girl who was walking through the hallway
of her home, and she came to the place where they had a
cellar door. It was one of those trapdoors on hinges, and it
was open. She looked down into the darkness, heard a noise
down there, and she said, "Who's down there?"

And her daddy said, "It's me, Daddy."

She replied, "Well, I want to come down there with you."

He answered, "Well, I've already taken the ladder away,
but if you'll jump, I'll catch you." Now this was a little girl,
and she thought, *Jump down into that hole?* You see, her father
could see her because she was in the light, but she could not
see him because he was down there in the darkness, and she
said, "But, Daddy, I can't see you."

He answered, "That's all right, I can see you, go ahead
and jump."

"But, Daddy, I'm afraid."

"Now, Honey, wait a minute. I want to ask you a question.
Do you believe I'm down here?"

"Sure, I believe you're down there. I'm talking with you."

"Do you believe I'm strong enough to catch you?"

"I believe you're strong enough to catch me."

"OK," he said, "do you believe that I love you?"

"Yes, Daddy, I believe you love me."

He asked, "Have I ever told you a lie?"

"No, you've never told me a lie."

"OK, you know I'm here, and I love you, and I would
never lie to you. Now jump."

And she said, "OK, Daddy, here I come." She stepped off
into that black hole, and her daddy caught her, gave her a
hug, and sat her down.

Believe it or not, that's what faith is. "Whom having not
seen, we love." We know God is there. He speaks to us
down inside. We recognize He cannot lie. We believe in His
strength, and we know He loves us. So, when He says "go,"
we go. When He says, "jump," we jump. When He says

"leap," we leap. This is what Abraham did. He stepped out onto the omnipotence of his Heavenly Father, and that's not a bad place to be. Are you willing to step out this moment on the omnipotence of God and to rest in Jesus?

Theologians and philosophers have concocted thousands of definitions of faith. *Abraham believed God.* There it is—plain, simple, unadorned. He believed the person of God Himself. He took God at His Word, at face value. That is raw faith. Faith is believing, even though not seeing. Faith is stepping out where there seems to be nothing and finding that Solid Rock beneath. John Greenleaf Whittier wrote:

> Nothing before, nothing behind;
> The steps of faith
> Fall on the seeming void, and find
> The rock beneath.

Notes

1. Herschel H. Hobbs, Ronald K. Brown, Compiler, *My Favorite Illustrations* (Nashville: Broadman Press, 1990), 260.
2. Charles L. Wallis, *A Treasury of Sermon Illustrations* (New York: Abingdon Press, 1950), 116.
3. Hobbs, Ibid., 42.

5.

Stop Trying—
Start Trusting

Hebrews 11:8; Genesis 12:1-4

*Now the Lord had said unto Abram, Get
thee out of they country, and from thy kindred,
and from thy father's house, unto a land that I
will shew thee. Genesis 12:1*

"By faith Abraham, when he was called to go out into a place which he should after receive for an inheritance, obeyed; and he went out, not knowing whither he went" (Heb. 11:8). God spoke to Abraham, and Abraham obeyed. Although he had no idea where he was going, he answered "yes" to the call of God in his life. There are only two kinds of people— the saved and the unsaved. There are only two qualities of life—a life according to faith and a life by sight.

Most people on earth live according to what they can see. What they don't see, they don't count on. So the world claims, "Seeing is believing. If I can't see it, then it's not the truth." Occasionally we may fall behind in the finances of our own church, and people might have the tendency to comment, "You see, we're falling apart. We have no hope. We've lost our way." Yet, those statements often spring from the mistaken notion that seeing is believing. In other words, if the financial statement is not all they expected it to be, then they feel there is no hope. They would then be defining faith as "seeing."

On the other hand, there is an uncommon, extraordinary way to live. That is to live by faith—to base your life primarily upon those eternal, invisible verities you cannot see. The world repeats, "Seeing is believing," but God counters: "Believing is seeing." We believe, and thus we begin to act on those truths we believe. The result is that God will open our eyes of faith to see "great and mighty things, which thou knowest not" (Jer. 33:3b).

God wants us, under His guidance and leadership, to chart a course. He wants us to plan our pathway with intense prayer, thus searching His mind and heart. He wants us to plan an annual budget as families so we will have a framework within which to work. That is also true with the church. As a budget is planned and adopted by a family and a church, God wants us to covenant, "Lord, now with Your help and by Your power, with the desire which we have in our own hearts personally, we are going to give generously to Your glory. We are going to give at least a tithe, 10 percent of all we make through the church to carry the gospel around the world. Lord, we are going to trust You to undergird us as we meet the needs of our church and this community." So, we begin to pray and to live on the basis not of the seen but primarily of the unseen—that which we live by according to faith.

Abraham Saw the Invisible

Silent—I climb the anguished dark,
Still I can hear a heaven-bound lark.
Sightless—I see! And, seeing, find
Soul-vision though my eyes are blind!
—Fanny J. Crosby

The Bible emphasizes from beginning to end that we must live basically on what we cannot see, and that is faith, whereas the world lives on the senses—sight, touch, taste, smell, hearing. As the people of God we are to live by faith, not only in the context of our church fellowship but also individually. For instance, you may be behind in your personal finances. Whatever your need, the Holy Spirit of God has far more power and more vast resources to meet your need than you ever will because God will expand on all you can possibly do. *But only as you trust Him.*

Perhaps you have another need in your life. Maybe there is an impending divorce or separation, and your heart is broken. The adjustments have been severe, and in agony you

STOP TRYING—START TRUSTING **73**

have reached out in every possible direction. You seem to be defeated by helplessness because all you view is darkness. It is as if there is no openness at the end of the tunnel, but there is help for the helpless, because in our helplessness we find the hope we desperately need. Jesus Christ will meet every need you have. He may not meet them exactly like you would prefer; He may not meet them precisely according to your time frame, but He *will* provide for your need. If you will trust Him, Jesus will bring hope in the midst of your hopelessness.

When we meet our friends at church we often ask, "How are you feeling?" But if we strictly followed the New Testament, we most likely would inquire, "How are you faithing?" It is infinitely more important how we are *faithing* than how we are *feeling*. In the final analysis, it is not your feeling that counts the most—it is your faith. When we believe God we link our finitude and weakness with His infinitude and Almighty power. Faith is based on what God can do, and God can do anything!

Hebrews 11:8 keys in on the fact that, by faith, Abraham obeyed. His life was totally characterized by faith. As we continue to study Abraham, we become aware that, though he would sometimes tend to walk by sight, he would snap back to walk by faith in the unseen. The Bible does not claim that Abraham was perfect, but here in Hebrews the overview of his life demonstrates he was a man who lived by faith.

Now what is faith? Faith is *submission*. Abraham explicitly followed the instructions of God. Therefore, he had a faith which was submissive. In Genesis 12:1-4 we read, "Now the Lord had said unto Abram, Get thee out of thy country, and from thy kindred, and from thy father's house. . . ." We will learn later to what degree Abraham was able to respond in faith. He heard the voice of God and was willing to obey His will. ". . . Unto a land that I will show thee. And I will make of thee a great nation, and I will bless them that bless thee,

and curse them that curseth thee: and in thee shall all families of the earth be blessed." So what did Abraham do? "So
Abram departed, as the Lord had spoken unto him; and Lot
went with him: and Abram was seventy and five years old
when he departed out of Haran."

The Foundations of Faith

> How firm a foundation,
> Ye saints of the Lord,
> Is laid for your faith
> In His excellent Word!
> What more can He say
> than to you He hath said,
> To you who for refuge
> to Jesus have fled?
>
> —John Rippon

Of course, it was not Abraham's plan to leave Ur of the
Chaldees and then Haran and eventually settle in the land of
Canaan. When he left he had no idea where he was going, but
God had called him. God alone knew what He had in store for
his servant. Faith is following God, answering His call.

What is faith founded on? It is not founded on personal
motivation. Sometimes we have the idea in walking by faith,
If only I could get motivated. If only I could just think positively.
We live in a society where "positive thinking" is often pro-
moted as the answer to all our problems. I believe a Christian
ought to think positively, but I also believe if all we do is
think positively, we have short-circuited what faith is all
about. Faith does include positive aspects. When God possesses
a person's life, he is going to have a positive outlook about
what should be done for the glory of God on this earth. A
born-again believer should not be negative. Yet, positive
thinking is not enough. Now there are times when a person
will determine, as a result of his own personal motivation,
that he is going to do this or that. That is not faith. Rather, it
can be presumption.

"And they said [the people building the Tower of Babel], Go to . . . let us build us a city and a tower whose top may reach unto heaven" (Gen. 11:4). Those prideful people were going to build a tower to heaven, but no matter how high you may reach, God still must reach down to you. "And let us make a name, lest we be scattered abroad upon the face of the whole earth." Note there are four references to "us" in Genesis 11:4. "Let us, build us, let us, make us." Are you surprised that God rained down confusion on them? Is there any wonder God scattered them? They could do nothing worthwhile for the glory of God because they were obsessed with making a name for themselves.

Pay attention to the difference between that verse and Genesis 12, beginning with verse 1.

> "Get thee out of thy country . . . unto a land I will show thee. And I will make of thee a great nation, and I will bless thee, and make thy name great; and thou shalt be a blessing. And I will bless them that bless thee."

God's people will never take the first step of faith if they are determined to holler, "Us, me, us, me." Our only hope is to respond in faith to God Almighty, who says, "I will, I will. I will show thee, I will make thee, I will bless thee, and then I will bless them that bless thee." Four times in Genesis 12, "I will, I will, I will, I will." The difference between failure and faith in the Christian life is man's "let us" and God's "I will."

Responding to God's Revelation

Sir Thomas Browne, an eighteenth-century British believer, declared: "I bless myself that I never saw Christ or His disciples. I would not have been one of those Israelites that passed through the Red Sea; nor one of Christ's patients, on whom He wrought His wonders: then had my faith been thrust upon me: nor should I enjoy the greater blessing pronounced to all that believe and saw not."

Faith is not scheming up our own plans and expecting God to bless them. Faith is listening to God and trusting His "I will." Faith is not founded on personal motivation. We do not have the strength within ourselves to live a victorious personal life. We can do it only as we live by faith. Faith is not founded on personal merit or motivation. As I have pointed out Abraham had been a heathen idolater. Along with the people of Ur of the Chaldees he had no doubt worshiped the moon god. Young people should thank God for being reared in Christian homes by committed Christian parents. They have had the privilege of daily seeing the genuine Christian life. Some may rebel against it or forsake it, but someday they will say, "I thank God for my Christian parents." Abraham did not have the opportunity of growing up in a family which worshiped the Living God. In Joshua 24:2 is the statement, "And Terah, the father of Abraham, served other gods."

Maybe some of you had unbelieving parents while you were growing up. Perhaps they had nothing to do with God and His standards. If you have been born into the kingdom of God and you are a person of faith, you now can praise Him. "For by grace are ye saved through faith; and that not of yourselves: It is the gift of God" (Eph. 2:8). We are not saved by personal merit. There are many people who commend themselves to God by their church work, and yet they fail to have faith. If that has posed a problem for you, then God wants you to *stop trying* and *start trusting*. Romans 4:5 says, "But to him that worketh not, but believeth on him that justifieth the ungodly, his faith is counted for righteousness."

Faith is not founded upon personal motivation. Faith is not founded upon personal merit. Faith is responding to God's revelation to you and following His call in for your life's journey. Abraham was being separated from the worldliness of Ur and called to a strange country which was God's Promised Land. In Hebrews 11:8 we read, ". . . when he was called." That literally means "when he was being called." In other words, as soon as Abraham was called, he began packing. There was instant obedience. It may have required days to prepare or even months. But in his mind he was already en route. Maybe you are an adult, well into the pursuit of the goals and ambitions which you believe are right for your life. Could it be God has spoken to you and commanded, "I want you to turn loose and to go for my sake"? Then, from that moment on, if you fail to do what He desires, you will live in disobedience to the Lord, and your life will be miserable.

If God places a burden on your heart that your pursuits are not sufficient to God's glory and honor, and His voice speaks to your heart, then you have no real option but to respond, "Lord, I'll do it now." Some may alibi, "Well, I'm too old, or I don't have sufficient money, or my children can't be inconvenienced like that." Many have almost woefully confessed, "I believe God is speaking to me," and yet they struggle week after week and month after month. They hold onto the pew in front of them to keep from making a public declaration that God has called them. Remember that faith is *submission*. Faith is admitting, "No matter my age, no matter my station in life, no matter who I am today, I recognize that the most important element in my life is to serve God. If that is to continue to do exactly what I've been doing, or if God speaks to me to do something different, I will do that just as well—even if it is to go to a foreign country." Suppose God calls, "I want you; I want husband and wife; I want a family to become foreign missionaries for me"? What would be your answer?

Faith Is Submission and Separation

Dr. David Livingstone, one of the best-known missionaries since the New Testament era, testified: "I will place no value on anything I have or may possess except in relation to the Kingdom of Christ. If anything I have will advance the interests of that Kingdom, it shall be given away or kept, only as by giving away or keeping it I may promote the glory of Him to whom I owe all my hopes in time and eternity."

Faith is not only *submission*, it is *separation*. Abraham (Abram then) was heading out to a foreign country. To follow God means being separated from the world. For Abram it signified being separated from the world he knew as a boy. Abraham had to be set apart for God. You must, too.

As Christians we must understand that "worldliness" is not merely what we *may* do but more importantly what we *may want* to do. Satan has always tried to deceive the believer into thinking, *If I don't do it, then I'm all right*. No, you are not. Your attitude may be more significant even than your actions— wanting to sin, wanting to be selfish, wanting to engage in worthless pettiness. Worldliness can be an act, but primarily it is an attitude. It may be wanting man's praise, whether or not we receive it. It may be outwardly holding to high standards, while inwardly longing to live like the devil's crowd. It may be pretending to be godly, but motivated by selfish gain. Many people do not commit certain sins because they are afraid of the consequences. They might be caught. They might be arrested. They might catch a disease like AIDS or syphilis. They are afraid who will see them, or they wonder what others will think, all the while having a strong desire for sin. Let me remind you that the desire for sin is the root of worldliness, and the believer must be separated from such.

First John 2:15 says, "Love not the world, neither the things that are in world. If any man love the world, the love of the Father is not in him." When we long for the things of the world and when we operate with the modus operandi of the world, it often causes problems in our homes, in our work, in our church organizations. We insist we are going to do it in such and such a way when maybe it is not of faith at all but only by our organizational or planning whims. The world utilizes its own calculations. Yet we walk by faith. So not only is the act involved, the desire of one's heart to do that which may be sinful or worthless also enters in.

Abraham (I will call him Abraham most of the time) had no idea where he was going. Nothing made sense to him at first, and it did not have to make sense to others, either. As Abraham began to prepare for his trip to an unknown land, surely his friends asked, "Abraham, where are you going?" Now put yourself in his place. You have answered yes to this God, and He has called you to a strange destination.

Then they press you, "Where are you going?" So you answer, "I dunno."

Then they want to know "Well, how long you gonna be gone?"

"I don't know."

They inquire, "Whatcha gonna do when you get there?"

"I don't know." Then some smart aleck is likely to chortle. "I know where you're going. You're going crazy!"

Abraham replied, "No. God called me. I don't understand it, but I'm going to follow His call anyhow."

The world claims that seeing is believing, but the Bible teaches that believing is seeing. And God said, "Abraham, you go, and I will give you this land, and I will make you a great nation, and I will bless you and make your name great." The Tower of Babel made God angry. The people were going to make "a name for themselves," but God promised Abraham, "I'm going to make you a great name; I will show you; I will make you a great nation" (see Gen. 12:2). Was there a contradiction between God's attitude toward the people of the Tower of Babel and toward Abraham? No, there was no contradiction. God is not against greatness as long as He is the architect of it. "He resisteth the proud and giveth grace to the humble" (1 Pet. 5:5). In Luke 16:15, Jesus rebuked the Pharisees, "Ye are they which justify yourselves before men; but God knoweth your hearts; for that which is highly esteemed among men is abomination in the sight of God."

Abraham Was Called in "Mid-life"

God promised Abraham a great name, but not before Abraham was ready. Although Abraham was seventy-five years of age, he first had to face testing and trials. He had another 100 years to live by faith. God may be calling you to a career change. I watched "20/20" one night on television. They did a story on the mid-life crisis. I thought since I am in mid-life, I had better find out what a mid-life crisis is. If curiosity killed the cat, I would die right away. I am more inquisitive than ever before; I am curious about what is going on in this world. The television show followed the path of an attorney who lived in Washington. He had a high profile and a most successful law practice. They had interviewed him several years before, and now had tracked him down and found him in a little town south of London. He had a farm with cows and chickens. He wasn't aware whether he was past his mid-life crisis, but he did know it had effected a change.

But what I have in mind is not a mid-life crisis. I do not care whether you are twenty-five, forty-five, or sixty-five. But I insist that wherever you are in your life, if God gives you the overwhelming conviction it is time to change your direction, to alter what you are or do in order that you can glorify Him, then the best you can do is start making ready. God delights in helping make men and women great for His glory, as long as *He* does it. You may think you are insignificant. When God calls, most of us in fact, have nothing going for us. God created the world out of nothing—*creatio ex nihilo*—and He continues to make people great who seem to have little or no promise. When God calls, you ask, "Can I know it?" Yes, you can, because when God calls, He calls with a spirit of conviction and persuasion, and you can know for certain. Paul was enabled to testify, "For I bear in my body the brand marks of the Lord Jesus."

Today, if you are bereft and directionless, you would do

well to pray, "Lord, in spite of the best intentions of my heart to hear your voice in my life, I still am confused. I shouldn't be in this kind of turmoil. So, God, I humble myself before you. Please speak to my heart and give me the sensitivity to hear Your voice and grant my spirit the desire to be obedient to Your will." And then God may well reach down and pick up a dentist, a doctor, a lawyer, a preacher, a secretary, a professional or non-professional in the community—and He will speak deep down inside, "For all you have been, I want to pick you up for My glory." Then you can answer, "I live for Your glory, Lord, in what I am doing if it is Your purpose for me." No matter what we are doing, we should have one purpose and one purpose only—to glorify Jesus Christ.

Abraham answered, "I'll go." So did Moses. So did Isaiah. So did Jeremiah. So did Peter. So did Paul. So did Stephen. Will you answer, "I'll go"? Abraham was ready to leave his home, even though he had no proof he was doing the right thing. Surely people around him jeered, "You're crazy." He headed for a strange country, but he was content. When God calls you, He may find you clinging to the thoughts and things of the world; floundering like a ship without a sail; or settled and comfortable with the station you have reached in life. He may even discover you unwilling to go where He wants you to go, but the life of spiritual vision possesses a faith which follows God's direction.

> Sweetly, Lord, have we heard Thee calling, "Come fol-
> low Me!"
> And we see where Thy footprints falling, Lead us to
> Thee.
>
> Then at last, when on high He sees us, Our journey
> done,
> We will rest where the steps of Jesus end at His throne.
>
> Footprints of Jesus that make the pathway glow;
> We will follow the steps of Jesus where'er they go.
>   —Mary B. C. Slade

6.

Finding God's Way

Hebrews 11:8-10;
Genesis 12:1-3; 17:5

And I will bless them that bless thee, and curse him that curseth thee: and in thee shall all families of the earth be blessed. Genesis 12:3

Real Christianity is considered an exclusive, dogmatic faith by the world. It proclaims the absolute truth that there is only one way to respond to God, and that is by faith. We have no hope except by faith. It is Jesus and Jesus alone. It is the Jesus way.

Abraham—Honored Around the World

Now with the exception of the Lord Jesus Christ Himself, Moses, and Paul, no other man has ever made a more profound impression on mankind than Abraham. The Muslims, the Jews, and we Christians respect Abraham. He is one of the most admired men who has ever lived, and nearly one-third of Hebrews 11 is devoted to this patriarch. He is mentioned in the New Testament no less than seventy-four times. He is the only person in the Bible who is called God's "friend" (Isa. 41:8).

In Romans 4:11, Abraham is called the "father of all them that believe." Abraham was great because he was a man of faith. In studying his life, we will focus on how to live by faith. Note verse 8 begins, "By faith." Did Abraham always have faith? Abraham grew up in a pagan home. Terah, Abraham's father, was not a godly man. In Joshua 24:2 it declares that Abraham's father worshiped "other gods." Abraham was once a pagan, but he became a believer, the "Father of Faith." His faith teaches us how to live by faith.

So what is faith? Faith is finding God's way. You may ask, "Well, how do we find God's way?" The revelation of God is God's Word to man. Faith is our response to that revelation. You cannot have faith until you receive the Living Word, Jesus. Then your faith grows through the Written Word, the Book, as you expose yourself to the presence of God and let Him begin speaking to your heart. You can learn about Jesus and not know Him. You can study the historical Jesus and not know the deep truths of the spiritual Jesus. You may have trusted in Jesus as your Savior, and yet you can be unwilling to walk by faith, because faith is finding the good and acceptable and perfect will of God. Jesus is the revelation of God to mankind through His Holy Word, and we must respond to that revelation. Until we saturate ourselves with the Word of God, until we listen to the spiritual Jesus, until we grow in the Spirit of God—until moment by moment, hour by hour, day by day, we learn the Word of God and live the Word of God, we shall not be practicing our faith.

God speaks, and as we respond to what He says, that is faith. There cannot be faith unless God speaks, and there is no faith until we respond. Romans 10:17 goes, "So then faith cometh by hearing, and hearing by the word of God." Unless you hear God speak there can be no faith. Faith is forsaking self and following Christ. We cannot live until we die. When we receive Jesus Christ the "old" man dies, and we are instructed to reckon ourselves as "dead." Romans 6:11 deals with reckoning ourselves dead. In other words, the Bible teaches if I'm going to live in Christ I must be dead to self. "Likewise reckon ye also yourselves to be dead indeed unto sin, but alive unto God through Jesus Christ our Lord."

Dying to Self

I am crucified with Christ: nevertheless I live; yet not I, but Christ liveth in me: and the life which I now live in

the flesh I live by the faith of the Son of God, who loved
me, and gave himself for me.

—Paul (Gal. 2:20)

"Knowing this, that our old man is crucified with him,
that the body of sin might be destroyed, that henceforth we
should not serve sin" (Rom. 6:6). Then absorb Ephesians
4:22: "That ye put off concerning the former conversation the
old man, which is corrupt according to the deceitful lusts."
We are to "put off the old man," that is, we are to die to self
and we are to live in Christ. You cannot live the faith life
without dying to self. Even though you are a Christian,
when you let self resume control of your life, you momentarily close the conduit of your heart through which you receive
the revelation of God and in turn respond to Him. So, you
are walking by sight and not faith.

When the Soviet Union existed, a true incident was
reported by the underground church in Russia. The Christians were excited as they looked forward to the new
section of the Gospel of Luke that had been received from
a secret home church in another city of the Soviet Union.
Since Bibles were so scarce, the churches took them apart
and exchanged pages with one another. It had required all
day for the local body of Christians to assemble. They had
to come in different intervals in groups of two or three at
the most, so they would not attract the attention of ever-
present KGB informers.

As they were about to sing in subdued volume their first
hymn of praise, the door burst open, and two Soviet soldiers
with automatic weapons rushed in. They ordered the con-
gregation up against the far wall. Then one of them demanded,
"Anyone who will renounce faith in Jesus Christ may leave
now. The rest of you remain with your hands up!" Two
left.

Then four left, and the soldier yelled in an even more
threatening voice, "This is your last chance to renounce faith

in Jesus Christ or face the consequences." The parents with children looked down at their frightened little faces, but no one else left. One of the soldiers walked over and slammed the door shut. Then they both put down their weapons and exclaimed, "Keep your hands up, but in praise to the Lord Jesus Christ, Brothers."

As the believers looked at them in total astonishment, the soldiers continued, "We have become believers through contact with other believers from home churches like yours. We were sent to arrest them, but we were converted to their faith, and through our previous experience we learned that no one can be trusted unless he is willing to die for his faith." This is an illustration of being willing to die physically for faith, but we must be willing to die to self before we are ready to live in faith.

"By faith Abraham. . . ." Of course, we have to study the Old Testament to learn about the life of Abraham. We ought to study the Old Testament to see what the New Testament is all about. By the way Genesis 17:5 reports that God changed his name from Abram to Abraham, for the word "Abram" means "father lifted up." The word "Abraham" means "father of multitudes," and we recognize that Abraham became the father of nations through his descendants. In Genesis 12 we read, "Now the Lord had said unto Abram . . . Get thee out of thy country, and from thy kindred, and from thy Father's house, unto a land that I will shew thee." Who was speaking to Abraham? The Lord. Do you believe God can reveal Himself to you today through His Word and through the leadership of the Spirit? Remember, faith is the revelation of God and our response to that revelation.

In the Word, God was speaking of His chosen people. When we think about prophecy and we view the Jewish people returning in vast numbers to Israel, as Christians we cannot possibly believe that the Old Testament will not keep its promises. The Word of God is true, and the prophecies of the Old Testament have come true, are coming true, and shall come true. When God promises, "I will bless a nation," those who curse that nation themselves will be cursed. God means exactly what He says.

The Confusion of Babel

Turn to Genesis 11:3-4: "And they said one to another, Go to, let us make brick, and burn them thoroughly. And they had brick for stone, and slime they had for mortar. And they said, Go to, let us build a city, and a tower, whose top may reach unto heaven; and let us make us a name, lest we be scattered abroad upon the face of the whole earth."

Notice the statements of those people, "Let *us* make brick. Let *us* build *us* a city and a tower whose top may reach unto heaven: and let *us* make *us* a name lest we be scattered abroad upon the face of the earth." There was a vast contrast between Abraham and the builders of the Tower of Babel. Pay attention to the difference in that portion and Genesis 12:1-3, where God said, "And I will make thee a great nation, and I will bless thee, and I will bless them that bless thee." So what is there? In Genesis, 11, the people insisted on their selfish will—they were obsessed with us." But in Genesis 12, God promised Abraham four times, "*I* will. The distinction between man's "let *us*" and God's "*I* will" is the difference between failure and faith.

Faith is not what we can promulgate and then expect God to bless it; faith is responding to God when He says, "I will, I will, I will, I will." That means there is no righteousness within us except that which comes by faith. So when God speaks, you listen. Keep your eyes on the Lord Jesus Christ. 2 Corinthians 5:7 observes, "For we walk by faith and not by sight." If you believe you will see the glory of God. God promised to Abraham, "I'm going to make your name great!" Abraham allowed God to do it *His way*. All genuine greatness is traced to one calling, the calling of God, the revelation of God. Even though Abraham had previously worshiped a moon god. Like all of us he had nothing with which to commend himself to God, yet God broke through the darkness of his mind and spoke to him—Abraham believed God. Faith is not a response to how good I am but how good God is. Long since the names of the Tower builders have been forgotten, Abraham's is great. What a blessing he has been to all nations. But God affirmed Abraham, "I'm going to make you a great name." "Is there a contradiction?" No. R. T. Kendall, minister of Westminster Chapel in London, has commented, "God is not against greatness as long as He is the architect of it."

If we think of "making a name" for ourselves we are fighting against God. Jesus rebuked the self righteous: "Ye are they which justify yourselves before men; for that which is highly esteemed among men is an abomination in the sight of God" (Luke 16:15).

Faith: The Clue to Pleasing God

In faith, one's automatic response to God should be the spirit conveyed by Sylvanus D. Phelps:

> Give me a faithful heart, Likeness to Thee,
> That each departing day Henceforth may see
> Some work of love begun, Some deed of kindness done,
> Some wand'rer sought and won. Something for Thee.

Look with me at Hebrews 11:6. "Without faith it is impossible to please God." So faith is responding to the revelation of God and to the Word of God. Can you testify, "By faith, I will respond to God speaking to me. Today I believe"? Jesus once challenged the father whose son was tortured by a demonic spirit, "If you can believe, all things are possible to him that believeth" (Mark 9:23). Do you remember what the father cried out? "Lord, I believe; help thou mine unbelief" (v. 24). Faith is our response, my response, your response to the revelation of God through His Holy Word which leads us straight to Jesus, and there is no other hope, there is no other way.

What can wash away my sin? Nothing but the blood of
  Jesus;
What can make we whole again? Nothing but the blood
  of Jesus.
Oh! precious is the flow That makes me white as snow;
No other fount I know, Nothing but the blood of Jesus.
—Robert Lowry

7.

Living in the Faith Dimension

Hebrews 11:9-10

By faith he sojourned in the land of promise, as in a strange country, dwelling in tabernacles with Isaac and Jacob, the heirs with him of the same promise. Hebrews 11:9

The Bible declares, "By faith Abraham. . . ." There is no other avenue to finding God's way and will except faith. You cannot work yourself into it, and you cannot prove it to others. All you can and need do is accept the Lord Jesus Christ as Savior and then walk by faith. "By faith, Abraham..."

Notice, ". . . when he was called to go out into a place which he should after receive for an inheritance, obeyed." The Word of God teaches us that faith is following His expectation. Once we have found His way by faith, we are to continue following that way by faith. Abraham, in responding by faith, was obedient to the Word of God to his heart.

Then the text states, "He went out, not knowing whither he went." Abraham understood that faith was responding to the revelation of God. I agree: faith is our response to the revelation of God. Abraham lived in the faith dimension; he understood he was to do what God instructed him to do, not necessarily what he could prove to his neighbor or what he could indicate in any other form or fashion of this world's standards. He simply did what God commanded. As the father of faith, he understood that he had to move by faith and faith alone. And, of course, because he acted on faith, it caused him to be remembered and renowned for that faith.

"By faith he sojourned in the land of promise, as in a strange country, dwelling in tabernacles," literally "tents" in the Greek. Abraham and Sara were living in tents with Isaac, their son, and Jacob, their grandson. Hebrews does not record how long it was before Isaac was actually born, but Abraham was simply accepting the promise of God that he was going to have a son. Abraham, by faith, trusted God in that promise, and thus the Scripture declares that "he sojourned in the land of promise, as in a strange country, dwelling in tents with Isaac and Jacob, the heirs with him of the same promise. For he looked for a city which hath foundations, whose builder and maker is God."

Called Out of Paganism

We often are preoccupied about our future when we ought to be caught up in our faith. When we have faith, we can trust in the One who holds the future. Now that it is extremely important for us to hear. When we trust by faith, we do not have to be troubled by the future. For when we trust by faith, we are relying on the very One who holds the future in His hands. You will remember that God called Abraham to "get thee out of thy country, and from thy kindred, and from thy father's house" (Gen. 12:11).

By faith Abraham left his pagan home country. He left his father and his godless kindred. God's call always insists upon separation. Even the word "church" comes from the Greek word "ekklesia," which means the "called out ones." So we, the church, are called *out of* the world to be *in* the world but not to be *of* the world. We are "called out." At any point when we come to believe by faith, the Bible makes it plain we are going to face separation. We will undergo separation from the world and from its standards when we live by faith. The Bible teaches that we are not living wonderful Christian lives merely because we are decent, upstanding, successful citizens. Many so-called "good" people are not godly. All that separates you as a born-again believer from the supposedly "good" person in the world is faith, not your goodness, because it is not yours but the goodness of God planted within.

Life in Abraham's day had degenerated. Generation after

generation had given no indication of trusting God. Years before at the Tower of Babel, the people had cried, "Let *us* build us a tower. Let *us*, let *us*, let *us*." This is what happens when our thoughts are on self rather than on our Savior; we will do exactly as they did, emphasizing self, "Let *us*, let *us*." They were more interested in what they thought than in what God thought. Abraham's call was to listen to the voice of God and this is what he heard: "Get out of this place!"

Only when we forsake the world's way and follow God's way will we ever walk by faith and not by sight. When we walk by faith, we are going to concentrate on the Lord Jesus Christ. Notice that Abraham was called out of a *place* to go into a *place* that he should "after receive for an inheritance." I want you to think with me about something. Had he been given the inheritance (the Promised Land) before he went out, no one would have ever questioned his sanity. If he had been granted the inheritance before he went out, the world would have observed, "Why, that's the logical thing to do. Go for the money. Run for the roses." They would not have doubted his senses if he had received the inheritance before, but neither would they have seen his faith.

The Bible reports that God called Abraham to break all ungodly ties, even with his father. When he set out he took a step of faith. He launched out to live in a new dimension— no longer by sight, now by faith. From Abraham's life we learn that if we are going to please God, we must *live* by faith and *look* by faith. Verse 9 states that Abraham entered into the land promised him, Canaan. But I want to focus in on a truth about that experience. We read how God promised it to Abraham. How excited Abraham must have been entering the Promised Land! Now I want you to put yourself in Abraham's place.

No Welcoming Committee in Canaan

When Abraham arrived in the Land of Promise, there was no welcoming committee sponsored by the Canaanites Chamber of Commerce. There was no banner which read, "Welcome, Abraham, to the Land of Promise." There were no bands playing; no choirs singing; no mayor to give him a key to the city. Abraham might well have asked, "Is that all there is?"

All he heard was the same voice with which he had become familiar. The same voice that instructed, "Get thee out," also said to Abraham, "This is it." You ask, how do you know that? Genesis 12:7 shows you. The Bible says, "And the Lord appeared unto him." When Abraham reached the Promised Land, there were no bands, no choirs, no fanfares, only God's voice. But that voice was enough! That voice meant so much to Abraham that he built an altar at a site near Bethel in order to thank the Lord.

Abraham lived by faith, not because of *what* he knew, but because of *Who* he knew. He knew the living God, the Creator of the heavens and the earth. He lived by faith as a pilgrim, daring to believe that God in His own time would make good His promise. He lived as an alien in a foreign land, and so do we when we have Jesus Christ as Savior. Today Satan is "the prince of the power of the air" and "the prince of this world." We are living in an alien world that has not yet been redeemed by the Lord Jesus Christ, and when Jesus comes again, the Bible prophesies that his old world is going to be redeemed—not only those who trusted in Christ, but this whole earth is going to change.

God's going to redeem it, going to bring it back. God gave it to man, but he failed. Man said "no" to God, and man said "yes" to Satan, falling into sin and death. Thus the world came under the dominion of the forces of this world and the cohorts of Satan. As we march through this world in these physical bodies, we are proceeding as pilgrims, parading as sojourners, passing through as strangers in a foreign land.

That was exactly what Abraham did as he dwelt in the land of Canaan. He lived by faith. All the rest of his life, Abraham traveled up and down the land which God had promised him, but he never owned more than a small plot in which to bury Sarah! Genesis 23 reports that when Sarah died, Abraham purchased from Ephron the Hittite a field sufficient enough to bury Sarah. Genesis 23:19 says "Abraham buried Sarah." That's the only plot he ever purchased in the Land of Promise. Yet, it was actually his by the grace of God.

Abraham Never Possessed the Land

There's a land that is fairer than day,
And by faith we can see it afar;
For the Father waits over the way
To prepare us a dwelling place there.

In the sweet by and by,
We shall meet on that beautiful shore;
In the sweet by and by,
We shall meet on that beautiful shore.
—Sanford F. Bennett

Though Canaan was a land of promise, it was never possessed by Abraham. Neither was it possessed by Isaac, his son, nor by Jacob, his grandson. They lived out their lives, according to Hebrews 11:9, in tents. Imagine it! These great patriarchs were in the land which God had promised, but they never settled down in it. They never possessed the land except by faith. You yourself will never possess this land except by faith. No matter what you may own, it is only God who owns the cattle on a thousand hills. This land is not our land. This land is God's land. I love the patriotism of the ballad "This Land Is Your Land." I'm grateful for the freedom we have in this nation. I am merely making the point that from a spiritual sense we must reach the place where we understand that this is God's land. These are God's possessions, and we are nothing more than pilgrims passing through, waiting for a homecoming with God, yearning for that dwelling place which has foundations whose maker and builder is God.

The promises of God require patience, but with patience

we can stand for God. Patience in the New Testament literally means "to endure." So when we speak of "the patience to
endure," we are giving it double impact—for to have patience is to endure, to endure is to have patience, and if we
are going to see the fulfillment of God's promises in our lives
this generation, we must have patience as Abraham did.

How was it that he had patience? He was a rich man, and
so it would be fair to ask the question, "Why didn't Abraham
just go into the Land of Promise, and instead of dwelling in
tents and going here and yonder, why didn't he just build his
own city? Why didn't he purchase thousands of acres of
land?" Because if he had done that, it would have ceased to
be the land of promise. Abraham was aware that when God
made the promise He did not have only a few acres in mind.
God had promised a vast land for His people.

What a pity it is when we sell ourselves short of the
ultimate will of God; when we, by our own actions in the
flesh, try to possess the land rather than allowing God to
give us the land, whatever the land may be in reference to
our lives. You never will be really settled in your life—there
will be a little bit here and a little bit there. The most
restless people in the world are those believers who have
settled for less than God had for them, those who sense
they have missed the will of God. In essence, they have
gone in and purchased the land that God had promised to
give them.

God Reserved the Land for Abraham's Descendants

The expression "the seed of Abraham" refers to three
separate entities. First, it obviously refers to the poster-
ity, the descendants of Abraham. It refers to the Hebrew
nation, the Israelite people. And the Lord actually swears,
saying, "I will bless thee, and . . . I will multiply thy seed
as the stars of heaven, and as the sand which is upon
the sea shore" (Gen. 22:17). So the seed refers first to the
descendants of the patriarchs, to the Hebrew people.[1]

When God made the promise, He covenanted it for Abraham's descendants. Faith is always dependent upon the Word of God. So when God spoke, Abraham listened and followed. Romans 10:17 notes, "So then faith cometh by hearing, and hearing by the Word of God." We ought to hear that verse repeatedly. There is no means of coming by faith except hearing the Word of God and obeying it. Abraham and his fellow believers were not without a word from God to cover their time of waiting, for the Almighty had already told Abraham he would die before the land grant of Canaan was made good to his seed.

Therefore, when God promised Abraham the land of Canaan, He prophesied it would be his descendants who would literally live in the land, who would be established in the land, and who would possess the land. He was saying to Abraham, "You are going to be a sojourner in the land," telling Abraham that his immediate descendants would leave the land, and in the will of God they would return in the fourth generation to receive the complete promise. If you want to read about it, turn to Genesis 15:13-16. The grandson of Abraham, Jacob, went down to Egypt, and the fourth generation from Jacob came back to the Promised Land, and who was the fourth generation after Jacob? Who was the man who led the Hebrews to the brink of the Promised Land? Moses. And Moses was the fourth generation after Jacob. Did God keep His promise? God kept His promise to the letter.

Although Abraham never settled in, he had all the benefits of the land itself. Only when we abandon our right to ourselves are we going to find ourselves. In Matthew 16:15 Jesus says, "For whosoever will save his life shall lose it: and whosoever will lose his life for my sake shall find it." Abraham lived in tents, he was detached from the land, but he had all he wanted and all he needed from it. I want you to remember that when we are the least attached to earthly things, we enjoy earthly things most. If you are driving yourself crazy in the pursuit of earthly things, you are not going to enjoy them. If you always covetously have your eyes on what *somebody else* has, you are not going to enjoy what *you* have. What God wants us to do is to be grateful that He is meeting our necessities. In meeting our necessities, as we trust in Him, He has promised that by faith our life will be abundant. For starters we'll be free of "keeping up with the Joneses." We don't need to keep up with the Joneses. We need to keep up with the promise of God.

Their Perpetual Pastime—Pitching Tents

Abraham lived as a nomad. He passed that life-style on to Isaac. What did Isaac do with it? He, too, dwelt in tents and passed this manner of life on to Jacob, and Jacob dwelt in tents. Actually, Abraham passed on to his son the greatest inheritance a father could ever bequeath—the promise of God! Fathers, listen to me. If you pass up the opportunity to give your children an understanding of spiritual truths and an opportunity to receive Jesus Christ, you have withheld from them the most precious inheritance of all. It is the only inheritance that shall be "from everlasting to everlasting." You can leave them a good reputation. The Bible teaches it is important to leave them a good name. You can leave them all the wealth of the world. What they will do is argue over who gets what. You can leave them this, you can leave them that, but nothing is everlasting except their faith in Jesus who is "the way, and the truth, and the life" (see John 14:6).

The faith your children see in you will be evident in their young adult years, and they will do it exactly like you. They will do more of what you did than what you said. So you must teach them by how you live as well as by what you speak. You fathers have the responsibility in your home to open the Word of God, read it to your children and to your wife, and lead them to God's house. You are the spiritual leader of your home. The downfall today is first in the home before it is anywhere else. What do I think about sex education in the public schools? If parents would be doing what they ought to be doing, we would not need sex education in the schools. In a Christian fashion we must teach our children that God created sex to be a meaningful relationship between a man and woman in the bonds of matrimony. We need to share with them what God's Word teaches about sex; if we teach them in the home and in the church, there will be no necessity to teach them in the public schools. In the public schools, you may on one hand have a splendid Christian teacher. On the other, you may have a person teaching so-called "safe sex" to your child, that is, teaching more "prevention" than all else. The only "safe sex" is God-ordained sex between a faithful man and true woman. Husbands, you are to be the tower of strength to your wives. Wives, you are also called upon to set a godly example.

Abraham lived by faith, and he passed that faith along to his children—then they came to trust in the same Living God. They received the greatest possible inheritance of all. We are to *live by* faith and then *look by* faith (v. 10). "For he looked for a city which hath foundations, whose builder and maker is God." The word "looked" in the Greek is translated "was looking," which means literally that Abraham eagerly expected to see an actual city. Abraham was a pilgrim in the Promised Land, but his eyes were on a reality beyond an earthly country. He was looking for the eternal city built by God for those with faith in Him.

What We Have in Common with Abraham

An unknown author wrote: "What Abraham sought on earth he did not find until he entered the portals of heaven. There never has been, and is not now, a city with permanent foundations. Our generation is certainly aware of this fact. Ancient cities with their thick walls and massive palaces required many centuries of disintegration. Today destruction and devastation are the rule rather than the exception in his hate- and war-torn world. The Christian pilgrim is sustained by God's promise to bring him at last to "a city which hath foundations, whose builder and maker is God."

Abraham's pilgrimage began exactly where ours must begin—with a vision of another and better country, a home forever blessed as the dwelling place of God. When did he look for that city? All the time! His eyes were fixed on that city, not for a while but all the time. His eyes of faith were riveted on that heavenly city. Faith sees things others cannot and do not see.

What kept Abraham going?

He was looking for the city.

What kept his patience in the face of an uncertain future?

He was looking for a city.

What kept him moving when he did not understand?

He was looking for a city.

What kept him beyond the petty problems of this world?

He was looking for a city.

We will begin to anticipate the promises of God only when our eyes are fixed on "the city which has foundations, whose builder and maker is God."

We will "turn the world upside down" only when we realize our mission—but in performing that mission, we must also stay fixed on that city. What a city! Abraham seems to have seen it first. "There's a land that is fairer than day, and by faith we can see it afar." He saw it from afar off, but one glimpse spurred him on. Tents, wealth, or mundane problems did not matter. What did? That city. Abraham recognized it was worth waiting for. It was the best inheritance to pass on to Isaac. Abraham could not have created it, for any city Abraham created would have had wicked people for its citizens. But he waited for a city which excluded the fearful, the unbelieving, and the abominable, the murderers, whoremongers, the sorcerors, the idolaters, and all liars.

Any man-made city would have included tears, death, sorrow, sickness, and pain. But he was looking for a city in which God would wipe away all tears from their eyes, where there would be no more death, neither sorrow, nor crying, neither any more pain, for the former things are passed away (see Rev. 21:4).

Abraham was looking for a city. Where did he expect to find it? Not on this earth, not in the sinful land of Canaan. Sure, he could have started his own city. He had the money, the family, the servants, 318 of them. But he had a different city in mind. A city with an eternal foundation, unlike the transient tents he pitched all over the Promised Land. When we set our eyes on things of the earth we live and die with every little thing that goes wrong. When we set our eyes on this earth, we live and die with those things which seem to pass too quickly.

That is why Paul advises us to put our eyes "on the things above, not on things that are on earth" (see Col. 3:2). When we focus on heaven and on Jesus, we are favoring God's way. Our focus is by faith and not by sight.

When I was seven years old, my eyes began to degenerate to the point were I could not see without correction. Today without my glasses or contact lenses everything is out of focus. My eyes are not too far from legal blindness, but with correction I have 20-20 vision.

This is what Abraham wants us to grasp—we must see life in the proper focus. When we come to God by faith, we begin to focus on Him and His city.

The old black spiritual tops it off:

> Oh, what a beautiful city!
> Oh, what a beautiful city!
> Oh, what a beautiful city,
> Beautiful city, Hallelu'!

Note

1. W. A. Criswell, *Welcome Back, Jesus!* (Nashville: Broadman Press, 1976), 70.

8.

When Faith Falters

Hebrews 11:8-10; Genesis 11:31-32

And Terah took Abram his son, and Lot the son of Haran his son's son, and Sarai his daughter in law, his son Abram's wife; and they went forth with them from Ur of the Chaldees, to go into the land of Canaan; and they came unto Haran, and dwelt there. Genesis 11:31

Those who have trusted Christ as Savior are sinners saved by grace. Nevertheless, Christians have to confront the fact that they sometimes falter in their faith. Sometimes we stumble, even if the desire of our hearts is to live completely for the Lord. Sadly, we do not always live up to the faith in us.

Many people think Abraham was nigh onto perfect. That's simply not so.

The Father of Faith Leaving Mesopotamia (Iraq)

"Men, brethren, and fathers, hearken; The God of glory appeared unto our father Abraham, when he was in Mesopotamia, before he dwelt in Haran" (Acts 7:2). So the Bible teaches that God called Abram (Abraham) while he was in Ur of the Chaldees (now Iraq). In Genesis 12:4, we read that Abram left Haran when he was seventy-five years of age. Now how long did Abram live? He lived to be 175 years old. Likely he was seventy years old when God first spoke to him in Ur (Gen. 12:1). So at that time he had over 100 years left to serve the true God who had revealed Himself to him.

Why do we struggle? Why is it that not all is copacetic? Let us investigate the factors of a faltering faith in Abram's life and ours. One factor is the *lack of perfection* (common to all of us) and another, *lack of patience*. God called Abram, and in Genesis 12:4 is the statement: "He departed out of Haran." Verse 5 records that "Abram took Sarai his wife, and Lot his brother's son, and all their substance that they had gathered, and the souls that they had gotten in Haran; and they went forth to go into the land of Canaan; and into the land of Canaan they came." Abram literally reached the land of promise. From obedience, he departed from Ur, and he and his caravan finally made it across the parched desert to the land God had promised.

Obedience Is Precious

Thomas Coke, one of Methodism's founders, at age sixty-seven obeyed God by accepting the call to become a missionary to India. He confessed, "I am now dead to Europe and alive to India. God has said to me: 'Go to Ceylon!' I would rather be set naked on its coast, and without a friend, than not to go!"

Hebrews 11:8 is absolutely right when it says, "By faith Abraham when he was called . . . obeyed." When God speaks to us, what does He want us to do? *Obey.* When our parents guide us, God wants us to do what? *Obey.* God spoke to Abram. How does He speak to us today? He speaks to us through His Holy Word and through the leadership of the Holy Spirit. It is little wonder so many Christians live a low-level life because they do not adhere to the Word of God.

The access to spiritual depth and being filled with the Holy Spirit of God, and to walk with Jesus, is daily to open the Bible and pray, "God, speak to my heart." Why? Because we lack perfection, and at times we are going to falter. We need to hear consistently God's intimate message to us.

So Abram responded with a first step of faith after God called him. Abram obeyed. It was that uncomplicated. Genesis 11:31-32:

> And Terah took Abram his son, and Lot the son of Haran his son's son, and Sarai his daughter in law, his son Abram's wife; and they went forth with them from Ur of the Chaldees, to go into the land of Canaan; and they came unto Haran, and dwelt there. And the days of

Terah were two hundred and five years [the father had a longer life than the son in this instance] and Terah died in Haran.

What had happened? Immediately appeared the reminder of Genesis 12:1: "Get out of your country, and leave your kinfolks, leave your father, and go into the land I will show you" (author's paraphrase). And what was the name of that land God would show him? Canaan. But where do we find Abram in 11:31? Haran. Not only was he there, his father, Terah, and the rest of his family were there. It appears from the text that rather than Abram taking his father with him, at least providing a form of leadership, Terah took Abram with him. Abram for the moment was following his earthly father rather than his Heavenly Father.

The name "Terah," strangely enough, means "delay." When Terah left Ur with Abram, the pilgrimage between there and Canaan was delayed in Haran for at least five years—sinful procrastination about carrying out God's plans and purposes! Catch the scenario. Abram was bogged down in Haran until Terah died. Did Abram start out to do God's will? Sure enough. Abram set out toward Canaan, but he did not leave his father behind; neither did he leave his pagan country. Therefore, Abram had not really left his country, his father, or his kinfolks. He did believe in the true God but could have backslidden because of his moon-god-worshiping neighbors and kinfolks.

Abraham, the Father of Faith, Faltered Plenty

Did Abram falter in his faith? Yes. He had made the first step, but then he also made a five-year stop. It is no different today; we are not being totally obedient to God. Many of us are stopping in our Haran. Often when we hear the voice of God, we are still not being obedient to His Word. Sometimes we are going to falter, but it is also true that God demands our faithfulness and obedience. He wants us to move toward the ideal, and when we do, He will keep picking us up and moving us onward so we may experience a renewal of faith.

How can we overcome a faltering, lapsing faith? Repentance. What is involved in repentance? It is a part of forgiveness. A sense of remorse and an emotion of being sorry are not enough. You must implore, "Dear God, with all that is within me, when I come to you for forgiveness, I am asking in light of my repentance." Repentance is turning around and committing to doing differently from what we have been doing. It means to pray, "God, I have lived by the world's standards, but now I am going to abide by the standards of Your Word." We must determine as those who claim the Name of Jesus above every name, "Lord, I'm going with You." As the Hispanics would put it, "Vaja con Dios"—"Go with God."

Abram's problem was partial obedience. You cannot walk however you want out in the world and have victory. You can't do "your thing" and go your own way. Rather, you must covenant, "God, with Your help and Your Spirit within me, I'll be the person You want me to be. I will try not to depart from your patterns, but if I do, I'll ask Your forgiveness!"

In Christ you are saved and kept by the power of God, but maybe you've had a relapse, and you're asking, "What can I do?" Do what Abram did. Abram, like us, started, but then he stumbled. He was on the mountaintop, then down in the valley. One moment he was loaded with confidence and another, he was let down to confusion. Abram set out to live life in a new dimension of rejuvenated faith.

Moving Toward the Promised Land

"And Abram passed through the land unto the place of Sichem, unto the plain of Moreh. And the Canaanite was then in the land." Now once again Abram was on the move, headed to the Promised Land, separating himself from Haran. When was he able to do it? When his father died.

While in Haran, he was only partially obedient to God. This may sound harsh, but when you are partially obedient to God, you are actually altogether disobedient. You are either obedient or disobedient. Many of us may have children who tend to live by the letter of the law but still not by the spirit of the law. That's sort of the nature of children, isn't it? Children often strive to be obedient, but they still tend to be disobedient. The smallest of our children have those inclinations because they have a bent to sinning.

Abram was finally on his way. As he left Haran, he was growing in God's grace. "But grow in grace, and in the knowledge of our Lord and Savior Jesus Christ" (2 Pet. 3:18). We grow in grace one step at a time. Now faith does have the quality and characteristic of jumping into seeming nothingness but ends up in God's hands. You must trust Him that completely; once that truth is established, you are going to grow in faith one step at a time. "One Step at a Time, Sweet Jesus."

Abram reached Sichem which means "shoulder," a place of strength, "unto the plain of Moreh," which means "instruction." Here was a place where he could lean on God to draw strength. At the plain of Moreh he could listen for instruction. You never become too old to hear a word from God. If you are too old to do so, you are too old *period*. God wants to speak to us in all the seasons of life, asking us to be pliable and teachable. So Abram was drawing strength. The last of verse 6 mentions, "And the Canaanite was then in the land." When Abram looked into the Promised Land every place seemed to be in the grip of the ungodly. Abram, of course, wondered, *What am I going to do? How am I going to possess the land?* He did not try to reason his avenue into the land. He was finally willing to let the next step be in higher hands.

The Facets of Faith

It is one thing to believe *about* God; it is another thing to believe *in* Him.

—Thomas Watson

There are numerous facets to our faith. We are to walk by faith, live by faith, act by faith, and to praise and worship by faith. We are not simply to reason it out by ourselves. Abram worshiped (v. 8) and planted his feet on higher ground. Notice that he camped between Bethel and Hai. Bethel means "the house of God" and Hai, "a heap of ruins." How unusual that he camped between the house of God and a virtual heap of debris—symbolically camping between two spiritual worlds, which is what we all do in this life. We are camped between the house of God and the hellishness of this world. The world tugs us downward; God pulls us upward. In which direction are you going? What means the most to you?

When Abram reached Canaan, there was a famine. What should he have done? Whether or not it seemed reasonable, he should have insisted, "This is where God put me, and this is where I am going to stay, even if we starve to death." When there is a famine in the land, what are God's man and woman to do? They are to trust God. Don't ever doubt in the dark what God has shown you in the light. In the darkest moment of your life, stay with the light. There is no other hope. God had ushered Abram into Canaan, and the famine was no doubt a test. God would have taken care of him, but Abram took refuge in Egypt. Once again he failed to trust God.

Many a Godly Person Trips Over Reason

> Manlike is it to fall into sin
> Fiendlike is it to dwell therein,
> Christlike is it for sin to grieve.
> Godlike is it all sin to leave.

Like he did we often turn to human reason. Either we will live by faith, or we will depend on sight and our own reason. What Abram did is so like us. He trusted God to move him from Ur to Canaan, but he would not trust Him to take care of him when he reached his destination. We often trust God to save us but do not trust Him to feed us. Sometimes we trust him with our souls but not with our money. These contradictions are numerous.

These were junctures when Abram had a lapse in his faith, failure in spite of his faith. Now let me present a background. In Genesis 14, there was a pitched battle of the kings, which involved the kings of city states or areas— Shinar, Ellasar, Elam, Admah, Zeboim, and Zoar. And there were more! The account relates that the enemies of the kings of Sodom and Gomorrah overran those cities, and those kings fled to the mountains. When the enemy army invaded Sodom and Gomorrah and ransacked the city of "all the goods of the city," they also took Abram's nephew, Lot, with them. Abram was no slouch. He heard of the raid and the taking of Lot as hostage. So Abram armed his 318 trained servants to be soldiers and pursued the enemy armies who had Lot with them. He caught them, defeated them, and recovered Lot and all the goods. Not only was Abraham (Abram) a man of faith, the friend of God, but a powerful fighter!

Chapter 14 also reveals that Melchizedek, king of Salem and "the priest of the most high God," blessed Abram. Verse 14 says that Abram "gave tithes of all" to Melchizedek. The "father of faith" set the example for us about giving tithes. Abram also returned all of the goods he had recaptured to Sodom and Gomorrah. For a brief time he had an opportunity to visit with nephew Lot. Lot still chose to live in wicked Sodom. As Abram watched Lot return to Sodom, he must have scratched his head and wondered, *Is it in vain that I have recaptured Lot? That I have saved his life? Is he going to return to the life of wickedness in Sodom?*

Melchizedek, the priest of the most high God who had blessed Abram, had gone. In a sense Abram was alone, his mind flooded with memories. I can imagine that he was thinking about the time when he was with Lot's family.

Maybe he again heard the laughter of the boys and the giggling of the girls, and he was reminded that he had no children.

God's Instructions to Follow His Way

Genesis 15 relates that the word of the Lord came unto Abram in a vision, "saying, Fear not, Abram: I am thy shield, and thy exceeding great reward." So, in verse 15:1, there was the promise of God. The shield meant, "I am thy Protector." It meant the Lord God was the potential for Abram's future and ours.

Here Abram was honest with God. You do the same. Be honest with God. There was an old song that went "Be Honest with Me, Dear, Whatever You Do." Be completely honest. Don't try to cover it up. Confess and be cleansed and free. Say, "Lord, I ask forgiveness," and God forgives and forgets.

Abram expressed it, "Everything that has happened to me is wonderful. The fact You are my shield, and You are my exceeding great reward, is great. But there is also sadness in my heart." He was candid. He continued, "Lord, You have allowed me to accumulate all of this world's goods, but I have no one to serve as my heir. I do not have anyone to give my inheritance. I still have no child. Lord, I know You promised me years ago that I would have a son, but I am now eighty-five years of age. Your promise has not come to pass." Now remember Abram lived until he was 175 years old. But at eighty-five he still had no children, and the situation looked hopeless. What was God trying to teach Abram? That the promises of God are not accomplished in the flesh but in God's way and time.

In verse 4, God told Abram, concerning Eliezer, "This shall not be thine heir." The son was still coming. In verse 4 there was the reaffirmation of that promise. And then in verses 5 and 6, there was the plentitude of God. The Lord led Abram out into the open air of the "starry, starry night" and asked him to look up at the heavens. As Abram gazed in awe, God promised, "Your descendants will be as innumerable as the stars in heaven. So shall thy seed be."

No human can count the stars. In fact, even Christian astronomers believe that the Almighty God is continuing to create solar systems with countless stars. In His plentitude God asserted, "I have the power to make your descendants number more than all the stars of heaven." God wanted Abram to know that he was unable to do it, but his seed would be numerous because of God's power.

Verse 6 stated that Abram "believed in the Lord; and he counted it to him for righteousness." That has never changed. Romans 4:3 and Galatians 3:6 also bear out that if we will believe the Lord, we are counted as being righteous, not because of who we are, but because of Who He is. Abram was saved because he believed in God. He had faith. He walked by faith. We go around trying to be "so good" that the rest of the world misses the fact that we have been saved by the grace of God. There are many decent, upstanding, even noble individuals who are going to die and go to an eternal hell, without God—because all they see in us is "goodness." They cannot see enough distinction to help them realize there is a difference between us and them. We are not saved by our merit but by the mercy of God.

Failure in the Family

But in spite of Abram's faith, we read in chapter 16 about failure in the family of faith. There is a reaffirmation of faith in chapter 15. In chapter 16, however, there is a relapse into the flesh. And they are poles apart, reaffirmation of faith and relapse into the flesh. Abram and Sarai grew impatient. Chapter 16 reveals impatience in the flesh; it gazes into Abram's home and records an early instance of domestic strife. And in Genesis 16 there is the an illicit triangle— Abram, Sarai his wife, and Hagar, the "other woman." The situation was highly explosive. If you dressed Abram in a business suit and Sarai in a fashionable dress and you placed a provocative maid in their midst, you would not only be up-to-date with next week's soap opera, you would have a picture of modern life in thousands of American homes today. If 50 percent or more of the couples in America are being divorced today, that means that maybe 75 to 80 percent of the homes are either divorcing or in serious turmoil. That scares me. It may be that only 20 to 25 percent of the homes in all of America are stable homes that practice, preach, teach, and live traditional moral values from the Judeo-Christian ethic.

Just as there was impatience in Abram's faith, that is a principal problem today. Most people come for counseling already set on divorce as they head to the courts. Most of them come too late to us, but even then, they are impatient. A relationship that has broken down in ten, fifteen, or more years, they want to put back together in ten minutes. The main problem is the failure to wait upon God. Even secular psychiatrists or psychologists are shocked. One psychiatrist observed that we have come to the place where we are so caught up in fantasy about what marriage ought to be, from what we read and see in the media, that people who have really good marriages don't even know it. Our models are wrong. Our standrads are weak. And the least little deal begins to break down the marriage.

The Impatience of the Flesh

The problem was impatience in the flesh, and then the sinful suggestion of Sarai that caused indulgence in the flesh. I can imagine Sarai came to Abram about like this: "Honey, I've just made the most wonderful discovery. I've been reading the Code of Hammurabi. Abram, the Code of Hammurabi is legal in the land of Canaan and honored here, and according to the code, it would be OK for you to marry Hagar, my slave. Then, when a slave is born to her, I can legally make him my son, and we can get around the problem of my inability to have children. Then I can have a child by proxy." Newspapers and magazines have played up the role of "surrogate mothers." Articles have stated that "surrogate motherhood is not new." They have referred to this biblical instance. Articles have gone on to point out that the process has since been "refined" with artificial insemination. Then the mother and father do not even have to meet each other. So Abram listened to the voice of Sarai, and not to the voice of Almighty God, who had plainly promised the "son of promise."

We have to determine, Are we going to indulge in the flesh? Or are we going to follow God by faith? Sarai made the proposal of the flesh. Abram accepted it and had a sinful affair with his wife's handmaiden. Ishmael was born, and he was not the son of God's promise. He was not in God's plan. What you have pictured in this passage is an attractive slave girl, a legal loophole, worldly reasoning, and a carnal resolve. The result was an entanglement that has been unresolved for over 4,000 years. Ishmael became the father of the Arabs today and, in a sense, the father of Islam. Isaac continued the faith bloodline of Abraham and was the promised son of God and was born through the Hebrew bloodlines. Abram and Sarai's impatience has caused untold misery and strife for century upon century.

I do not believe the Bible teaches the eradication of the fleshly nature. All you can do with carnal flesh is to nail it to the cross, to crucify it. Put it to death. Paul testified, "I die daily." One of these days when Jesus comes again, He is going to grab that old flesh and deal with it fully and finally. But until then, the snares of the flesh will try to enslave us. Even though you have Christ as Savior, the "old man" will try to trap you. The flesh and the spirit are contrary and neither gets along with the other (see Rom. 7). There is a constant battle, and there is only one way to live by faith. That is to claim the victory in Jesus and to crucify the flesh.

Paul exulted, "But thanks be to God, which giveth us the victory through our Lord Jesus Christ" (1 Cor. 15:57).

Disobedience Is Expensive

In these verses, there was a price to be paid. There is always a price exacted for sin. Jesus paid the price to forgive us if we will confess our sins. When you think *I am going to walk in flesh instead of walking in faith,* you are going to reach a point of sin—and somebody is going to pay the price. If you are a Christian, Christ has already paid the price for your sinful life. He has washed it clean and has forgiven you. But even as a Christian, you can begin to live more by the flesh, instead of by faith. You cannot lose your salvation. You are a son or daughter of God. Yet, you will pay the price for your sin here in this life. When Hagar conceived, and as soon as it became apparent that she would become the mother of Abram's first child, there was trouble. Anytime you act according to the energy of the flesh, you are headed for trouble. We have all discovered that, haven't we? We are not perfect. We all struggle in our faith and must battle against the flesh. We often pray, "Dear Lord Jesus, please be my Helper. Oh God, I need Thee every hour."

The harmony in Abram's home was gone, not to be restored for sixteen or seventeen years, and then only at the price of a painful separation, when his son Ishmael had to be banished from the home for all time. Sarai's suggestion to Abram was unselfish. Sarai's suggestion to Abram was one of sacrifice, but it was a sacrifice done in the flesh. Sarai's daily price tags came in the form of Hagar's haughty look when she boasted, "I am the mother of Abram's first child." She rubbed it in. "I, a mere slave girl, not you Sarai, am the mother of this child!" Sarai soon regretted her proposal. Putting up with intolerance and rebellion, Sarai confronted Abram one day with, "It is all your fault. You are to blame." Sarai made the suggestion; Abraham had merely done what she told him to do, and now she laid the blame on him. What was Abraham's reply? "She's your handmaiden. You do with her what you want to."

Hagar—Victim of Circumstances

Sarai dealt harshly with Hagar. We can hardly believe it, because Sarai in 1 Peter 3 is lifted up as the model of a faithful, submissive wife, and yet now we see in her resentment, meanness, and spitefulness. Why? Because she herself had made a proposal in the flesh that opened the door for her maid to look down on her. Sarai became upset and showed her dark side. Her heart had grown bitter. She realized the emotional turmoil of a tangled triangle. The human heart can be very deceitful (see Jer. 17:9). When the heart becomes upset, whatever is inside is going to come out. When you upset a bottle of honey, what comes out? Honey! If you have left it there too long, then you dig it out. It has become a form of sugar. But it's still honey. If you upset a bottle of vinegar, what do you have? It does not matter what the bottle is. What matters is what's inside the bottle, and when it's upset, it only reveals what's already inside.

Verse 6 records that Hagar "fled from her face." That was only natural; every member of the house was acting naturally. Abram "acted naturally" as he went into Hagar; Sarai acted naturally in resenting her maid; Hagar acted naturally in running away; Hagar knew no better than to do the natural thing. Hagar was the victim of the entire experience. Because she was an unsaved Egyptian who knew nothing better than to do what her master and mistress commanded her to do. Abram and Sarai knew the living God by faith, and they should have acted *supernaturally.*

Had Sarai walked with the Lord in that hour, she would not have made the suggestion that brought resentment, bitterness, and heartache to her own life. Abram had the greatest remorse, for he had the greatest responsibility, Why? Because he had surrendered his headship to Sarai. Husbands, you are to carefully weigh your wife's counsel.

You are to put her counsel in the crucible of prayer. You are to respect and admire her advice. You are to listen closely and carefully, but you have a responsibility to carry that counsel lovingly, hopefully, and caringly to the Lord, praying, "God, lead me, help me, give me discernment. My wife has so many good suggestions, Lord. Is this one where her counsel is the right approach?"

Abram lost his spiritual leadership in the home, and he allowed Sarai to nag that unfortunate slave girl until she fled the home in frustration. Hagar had failed as a maid. Sarai had failed as a wife. Abram had failed as a man. As a result Hagar the Egyptian fled. What a tragedy! Abram and Sarai had an imcomparable opportunity to lead Hagar in the life everlasting. Yet Hagar was treated like a piece of furniture. She was used and abused. When she fled Abram's house her mind was filled with bitter thoughts about the treatment she had received and with a totally false impression in her mind about Abram's God.

When people live by you and with you, do they see your God? Do they see Jesus Christ? Do they see the light of the world, the bread of life? Whom do they see?

In this instance, Abram failed in his faith, following the flesh. Not only did he fail, he failed his wife. He failed all future generations because he fouled up the plan of God, even though God was able to override it. It has left dreadful turmoil to this day. He failed Hagar because he failed to be a witness in the faith.

You may believe that you cannot quite identify with Abram, the father of faith, even though he sometimes failed. Maybe you cannot identify with Sarai, even though she failed here in her faith. But maybe you can identify with Hagar. Maybe you think, *God's given up on me.*

God has not given up on you, whether you are in Abram's place, Sarai's place, or Hagar's place. When Hagar, heavy with child, fled from the house of Abram, the Bible records that she rushed across the desert of Sinai. She came to the wilderness of Shur on the frontier of Egypt, crossing there with a tear-stained face and a broken heart. She suffered with every weary step. Where was she going? She had been close to the living God and to knowing genuine faith. Now she was going back to Egypt, back into the world, back to a worse bondage, back to darkness, back to her pagan people and their dumb idols.

Before it was too late, before the gates of Egypt could close behind her forever, God stepped in. Aren't you glad that God stepped in at some point in your life? God loved Hagar as much as he loved Abram. "The angel of the Lord said unto her, Return to thy mistress, and submit thyself under her hands" (16:9). Can you imagine what a difficult decision that must have been?

But notice in verse 14, "Wherefore the well was called Beer-la-hai-roi; behold it is between Kadesh and Bered." That long tongue twister means "the well of him that liveth and seeth me." Right there in verse 14, I believe Hagar passed from death to life. She passed from eternal damnation into eternal salvation. She passed from her pagan past to her heavenly future. She experienced the presence of God Himself. The Bible says in verses 15 and 16 that she returned to the household of Abram. When Abram was eighty-six years old, Ishmael was born to Hagar.

God assured them, "I'm still Abram's God, and, Hagar, I will be your God, too." Will you let him be your God? Would you ask forgiveness of your sins and ask Christ into your life? Maybe like Abram you are already saved. Your faith does not have to falter or fail. Cling to Christ.

9.

Famine or Feast?

Genesis 12:10; 13:1-10

And there was a famine in the land: and Abram went down into Egypt to sojourn there; for the famine was grievous in the land. Genesis 12:10

Is your spiritual life a famine or a feast?

> And Abram went up out of Egypt, he, and his wife, and all that he had, and Lot with him, into the south. And Abram was very rich in cattle, in silver, and in gold. And he went on his journeys from the south even to Bethel, unto the place where his tent had been at the beginning, between Bethel and Hai; Unto the place of the altar, which he had made there at the first: and there Abram called on the name of the Lord (Gen. 13:1-4).

God's Word gives us food for faith. It is the nutrient for the believer, and we have to determine in our own lives if we are going to feast or face famine.

The Holy Spirit was revealed to Abraham (Abram until Genesis 17) although the Holy Spirit did not come in an abiding presence to indwell the hearts of believers until the Day of Pentecost. When Jesus ascended into heaven, He had promised that One was coming to abide in our hearts. At Pentecost, for the very first time in all of history, the Holy Spirit came to indwell permanently in the hearts of all who would testify, "Lord, I'm a sinner, and I'm in need of a Savior." Not only does God reveal Himself as clearly today as He did to Abraham, he reveals Himself even more clearly. Why? Because now the Holy Spirit is here to abide, and now we live on this side of the cross. We are well aware that Jesus died and gave His life for our sin.

Spiritually Satisfied or Starving?

Billy Graham has asked the question, "Why should you eat from the devil's garbage can when you could have a T-bone steak at the Lord's table?"

Using Abraham as an example, God is asking, "Is your spiritual experience one of famine or feast?" Is there a hunger in your heart for an experience with the Lord Jesus that will supersede all else in your life? Have you tended to drift away from the faith you once had? Is there famine in your heart as a Christian? Is there famine in your heart because you have never had faith in Christ as Savior? Is there still a void or vacuum in your spirit? When you trust Jesus as Savior, your spirit is made alive by the very Spirit of God. You may have a famine in your life and you may hunger and thirst after righteousness because you have never answered yes to Christ.

Maybe you are famished in your faith because, like Abraham, you started out in faith, even set up an altar to worship the Lord, and regularly attended the house of God. Do you know that all is right between you and God? Are you feeding on the unsearchable riches of the Lord Jesus Christ? The Bible teaches us that we are going to be spiritually impoverished or spiritually nourished. Just as we require food for physical nourishment, we must have food for spiritual nourishment, food for faith.

Abraham started his pilgrimage by faith, but he discovered, as we often will: if we are not careful we will find yourselves amid famine. When you falter in your faith, you begin to ask yourself, "What happened?" When you do, you'll discover exactly what Abraham did in Genesis 12. God had promised Abraham the land of plenty, of milk and honey. But what did he encounter when he reached the Land of Promise? He came face to face with famine in the land of plenty! Not only was there famine in the land, as a result of it Abraham himself had a personal famine.

Notice the features of a famine in your faith. *First of all, as there was with Abraham, there will be a loss of trust.* You will also lose time serving the Lord. You may also lose your testimony.

"And there was a famine in the land: and Abram went down into Egypt to sojourn there; for the famine was grievous in the land of promise, in the land of Canaan" (Gen. 12:10). Now Abraham had built an altar and had worshiped the Living God in the land of Canaan. He surely did not expect to encounter famine in the land. *Here I am,* he mused. *I stepped out on faith responding to the call of God, doing what God told me to do, and now here I am in the midst of a life-threatening food shortage.* Abram had walked by faith and lived by faith throughout. Yet, when the first real test of his faith occurred, guess what he did? He hotfooted it down to Egypt. The prophet warns in Isaiah 31:1, "Woe to them that go down to Egypt for help; and stay on horses, and trust in chariots, because they are many; and in horsemen, because they are very strong, but they look not unto the Holy One of Israel, neither seek the Lord!"

Don't Make an Alliance with the Devil

Egypt also spoke of an alliance with the world. Abraham's faith diminished in the process. He began his pilgrimage with, "God, I trust You with all my heart, soul, and spirit." Now Abraham was wavering. "I've gotten here to the Promised Land, the supposed land of plenty, and now that I'm here there's a famine. Lord, you didn't say anything about a famine." So, Abraham let down his guard and began to doubt the same God in whom he had tremendous trust when he had set out for the Land of Promise. Abraham looked around and reasoned within himself, *Well, I've been going with God. That's the desire of my heart, but it seems for the moment I'm going to have to take things into my own hands. I'm going to have to use my mind in this matter. I can see that we may starve to death if we stay here.*

What was wrong with that? God had promised, "You go to the Land of Promise, and I shall provide." Now as the father of faith faced his first serious test, he protested, "God, you've led me to this land, but I don't believe You're going to provide." By his very actions he was not trusting God for provision. Woe to the believer who claims, "I'm going with Jesus," but when the famine comes, he heads to the world for help. Abraham did that. He turned his eyes away from the Lord, put them on his circumstances, and reasoned, "Well, after all, God expects me to use my head." But far more important is using our hearts. And when you live by and trust by faith, God will transport His Word to your head.

He Went Down into Egypt—Sinking Spiritually

When Abraham went down to Egypt, he disobeyed the Lord. The whole time he was in Egypt, he was out of the will of God. Why? Because he disobeyed and displeased God. Anytime you disobey God, you are out of His will. When you are out the will of God, the time you spend is going to amount to nothing—zilch. You cannot be out of God's will and expect His blessings to be poured out on your life. When your trust is on the wane, you are going to be marking time at best. At the judgment seat of Christ anything done out of God's will be like wood, hay, and stubble to be burned up (see 1 Cor. 3:11-15). But when you are in the will of God, your reward in heaven will be assured, spoken of as gold, silver, and precious stones.

When Abram went down to Egypt, one of his first moves was trying to deceive Pharaoh. He denied that Sarai was his wife in order to "save his own skin." When we lose trust in God and have a famine of faith, we begin to think more of our security than we do our testimony for the Lord Jesus Christ. Abram ruined his testimony to an unbeliever. He dishonored his Lord, even disgusted Pharaoh. When Pharaoh discovered that he had lied, he expelled Abraham and his family from the land.

What a shame and disgrace to our Lord when an unbeliever would complain to a believer, "You are dishonest and have caused tremendous trouble." When we are not living for God with a pure heart and a sweet spirit, we might as well do God a favor—do not attempt to witness. Even if you open your mouth and speak the name of the Lord, such will not have the blessing of the Almighty and the moving of the Spirit of God that results in changed lives.

Convincing Arguments for Christianity— Godly Christians

Though an able speaker charms me with his eloquence,
I say, I'd rather see a sermon than to hear one, any day.
                              —Edgar A. Guest

The greatest argument *for* Jesus is the life of a Christian, but conversely the greatest argument *against* Jesus is the life of some Christians. Abraham had a relapse of faith. So many of us do. Many members in churches I have pastored have prayed, "Lord, I want to be used of You. I want to be drafted into Your service. I want to be Your person, I want your Spirit to move mightily in my heart." That is wonderful. That kind of commitment is pleasing to God. The Bible commands that we become Spirit-filled Christians, absorbed by the Spirit of God. God wants us to feast in our faith. God wants us to have food for our faith. We must yearn for a feast of fellowship with God.

We will have no sweeping revival until the people of God come before Him and plead, "Oh, dear God, I want Your Spirit to rule and reign in my own heart for Jesus' sake." No church will have genuine unity until the people of God are so Spirit-filled they become witnesses for the Lord Jesus. Hardly a one of us can let time pass without thinking of a relative, neighbor, or friend who is doomed to hell and destined to damnation because they do not have Christ as Savior. What happened after the Spirit of God came down at Pentecost? Three thousand souls were saved. All the rest was secondary.

Carrying Out the Commission

God's people will be unified when their hearts are so filled with the Spirit of God that they will look at the lost world and be so burdened for their neighbor or friend and say, "Oh, how I prayed for that person to be saved. God, use me for that person to be saved." In Christ, we should come together and in every church experience, in Sunday School classes, in every organization, in our individual lives, and out on the street, people would recognize our rejoicing in the greatness and power of our Lord. Anything less than that is of the flesh and not of God. God gave us a mandate in the Great Commission to go, go, go, whether it be my church, a church across town, or a church around the world. Revival will be ignited among Spirit-filled people who become living, dynamic witnesses for the Lord.

When Abraham went down to Egypt and out of the will of God, he was no longer a proper witness for Christ. He entered Egypt a saved man but came out and returned to the altar of God as a Spirit-filled man, one who was sadder and wiser, for he had lost his testimony. He not only lost his testimony to the unbeliever but also to the believer.

Lot was Abram's nephew also justified by faith, but Abram was a more mature believer. Yet Abram took Lot to Egypt with him and also brought him out. Abram got Lot out of Egypt, but he never got Egypt out of Lot! When Abram was able to overcome, Lot was never able to overcome because he was a weaker believer, and it was his ruin on earth. Lot brought with him out of Egypt something more than herds and flocks. He had acquired a taste for the world. Abram was generous and magnanimous, but Lot was greedy and worldly. Abram "looked for a city whose builder and maker was God," but Lot made his home in a city that was built by man and destroyed by God.

Worldly Lot Knew Better

Many of us Christian men had better be grateful God doesn't turn our wives—or ourselves—into pillars of salt. All too often we are looking back to our sinful past. Genesis 13:10 notes, "Lot lifted up his eyes." That is, he had come to prefer to walk by sight rather than by faith. How impossible, then, for Lot to remain with Abram! How could those two walk together except they be agreed? Verse 6 explained, "They could not dwell together." In Genesis 13:12 we find that "Lot pitched his tent toward Sodom." What happened to him? He lost his family: he lived in disgrace. We always blame Lot for pitching his tent toward Sodom, but it wasn't altogether his fault. How do I know? Look at Genesis 13:10. Toward the end of that verse it says, "And Lot lifted up his eyes, and he saw a land like the land of Egypt." When Lot saw Sodom, he said, "Wow, that land looks a lot like Egypt."

You see, Abraham was able to overcome the famine in his faith, but Lot was never able to do that. You may be able to overcome the famine in your faith, but there are weak Christians who are going to be forever hurt in their journey because they've been down to Egypt.

Thank God the Bible doesn't end with Genesis 12. It moves into Genesis 13, and we learn about the feast of faith. The Egyptian experience was over. Abram had crossed over into the Promised Land. No doubt he decided he was never again going to step out of the will of God, God being his helper. He emerged from Egypt a spiritual man.

In verse 1 of chapter 13 there was a *severance*: "And Abram went up out of Egypt." Abraham had undergone a relapse of his faith, but now he had returned to his in-depth faith. Listen to Isaiah's message: "Let the wicked forsake his way, and the unrighteous man his thoughts; and let him return unto the Lord" (Isa. 55:7). So God would ask us, "Are you willing to forsake Egypt? Are you willing to cease your dependence upon the world?" Abraham was relieved he did. There are pleasures in sin but only for a season because there is no joy in sin. Do you know why there is no joy in sin? Because there is no salvation in sin, but there is a certain pleasure in sin, or people wouldn't sin. And yet the most miserable person on earth is not the unsaved person. The most miserable person on earth, I believe, is the saved person who is out of fellowship with God. I believe Abram started out for God and then went down to Egypt. He was miserable because he had God in his heart and Egypt under his feet, and he was unhappy in both worlds. You will never know joy until you leave your Egypt and return all the way to the Lord.

Second, there was *setting apart* as shown in verses 2 and 3. Severance and setting apart are two sides of the same coin. Setting apart or sanctification is not so much separation "from" as it is separation "to." It is not merely leaving Egypt, it is going all the way back to Bethel. Abraham went to Bethel. Bethel means "the house of God." Abraham returned out of Egypt, out of the land of sin, back to the house of God. Being set apart is putting as much distance between you and the world as you possibly can.

I heard Fred Wolfe, pastor of Cottage Hill Baptist Church, Mobile, tell about a woman who wanted to hire a new coachman. She had three applicants and interviewed them one at a time. She questioned all three. "You know that steep hill just outside of town and that narrow stop where the road drops away to the ravine? How close could you drive my coach to the edge without losing your nerve?"

The first man replied, "Madam, if the wheels of the coach came within six inches of that edge, I would feel quite safe."

The second answered, "Madam, I reckon, even if one of the wheels went clean over the edge, I could hold those horses and recover the coach without harm."

The third coachman was hired. His answer? "Madam, I would keep the coach as far away from that ravine as I possibly could."

Sanctification is staying as far away from the world as you

possibly can. The Christian is to be in the world but not of the world. It is not trying to come as close as you can. When you get as close as you can, there is the possibility of losing your testimony. Even though we are to witness to those in the world, sanctification is keeping as far away from the world as we can which will allow us to come as close to God as we can. There are severance, setting apart, and sacrifice in the feast of faith.

The account says that Abraham "pitched his tent... and builded an altar unto the Lord" (12:8). Then Abram came back to the altar (see 13:4). His tent was symbolic that he was a pilgrim in this world, simply passing through. We are all pilgrims... just passing through. Unless the rapture occurs soon, all of us are going to die sooner or later. He lived in a tent, but he built a permanent altar which showed he was trusting God with all his heart and soul. He came back to that altar, and the Bible indicates that Abraham beheld the gospel. God revealed to him long ago that Jesus would come, die, and be resurrected. Galatians 3:8 indicates, "And the scripture, foreseeing that God would justify the heathen though faith, preached before the gospel unto Abraham, saying, In thee shall all nations be blessed." Jesus said, "Abraham saw my day and was glad."

Every altar in the Old Testament is a promise and a prophecy of the day that Jesus would enter this world and die on the cross. He is the Lamb of God who takes away the sin of the world.

If there is a famine of faith in your heart, why not depart from Egypt? Why not return to God and let God proceed with your sanctification? Why not claim your relationship with the Lord Jesus and the sacrifice that Jesus made for you? The blood of Jesus cleanses us from *all* sin. God took Abram back. He will do the same for you, too.

10.

Fulfillment in the Family

Genesis 21:1-14

And the Lord visited Sarah as he had said, and the Lord did unto Sarah as he had spoken. Genesis 21:1

And the Lord visited Sarah as he had said, and the Lord did unto Sarah as he had spoken. For Sarah conceived, and bare Abraham a son in his old age, at the set time of which God had spoken to him. And Abraham called the name of his son that was born unto him, whom Sarah bare to him, Isaac. And Abraham circumcised his son Isaac being eight days old, as God had commanded him. And Abraham was a hundred years old, when his son Isaac was born unto him (Gen. 21:1-5).

You may remember that Abraham lived to be 175 years old. Nevertheless, 100 years of age was rather old in that day. Abraham and Sarah were past childbearing. We are reading about a miracle of God. "And Sarah said, God hath made me to laugh, so that all that hear will laugh with me. And she said, Who would have said unto Abraham, that Sarah should have given children suck? for I have born him a son in his old age. And the child grew, and was weaned: and Abraham made a great feast the same day that Isaac was weaned" (vvs. 6-8).

The name "Sarah" springs from the Hebrew root which means literally "to persist." Sarah gave birth to Isaac, the promised son, when she was ninety. In spite of the fact that they had been far from perfect, they were noted for their faith, for they knew salvation as God revealed Himself in that day. They had walked by faith, but, like us, they had failed at times. And as a result of that failure, Ishmael was born into this world.

But Sarah lived up to her name, for she was persistent. She stayed in touch with God; at the advanced age of ninety, the very promise of God came to pass in her life. I could not help thinking that "to persist" is an important interpretation of the name Sarah. My wife, Jodi Chapman, is actually named *Sarah* Jo. She, too, matches her name. She has persisted and persevered. She, too has stayed in touch with God through the years. I praise God for her love and strong faith that have supported and encouraged my heart.

Here is recorded the miracle birth of Isaac. Faith is exceedingly powerful. That is the major lesson God wants us to learn from this passage. Faith is the greatest power on the face of this earth, and there is no greater power. One word for power in the Greek New Testament is *dunamis*. From this we receive the word dynamite, TNT. Faith spiritually explodes in our lives when we experience the grand grace of God. We realize that God is above all, over all. He is *omnipotent*. He is eternally powerful. We come to know Him through the Lord Jesus Christ, God-man. Faith is more powerful than all the atomic weapons in the world. Why? Because faith sees the invisible. Faith not only sees the invisible, it hears the inaudible. Faith not only sees the invisible and hears the inaudible, but faith accomplishes the impossible.

The Incredible Power of Faith

> Lord, as of old at Pentecost
> Thou didst Thy pow'r display,
> With cleansing, purifying flame,
> Descend on us today.
> —Charles H. Gabriel

The Bible makes it clear that when we know God, He wants to perform the impossible through us. When dynamite faith enters our lives, we are going to respond constantly to that faith. In essence, you will pray, "God being my helper, I will allow Your Spirit to move through my life."

If you want to see the *possible* happen in your life, then do it on your own hook. Many positive developments can happen and certain successes can come, even in the lives of the unsaved. But it is only by faith that one will ever see the impossible occur. Christians often ask themselves, *I wonder why I don't see more of God's power in my life.* It is because God is waiting for them to have faith enough that He might unleash that incredible power. When we step out on the limb of faith, then God is ready to do the extraordinary, the supernatural, that which the world cannot comprehend—except when they view it through our lives. Faith accomplishes the impossible.

Down in our souls there is an intense longing to sense that power in plentitude, and God has made it available. If we do not know it, it is because of our own lack of faith. "O ye of little faith!" our Lord cries. For he wants us not to walk by our own reasoning. We must walk by the revelation of Him from above and within. Tragically, to certain people, faith is all talk and no walk. People who talk about faith but don't walk by faith are rather powerless persons. They may have the beginning faith to trust in Christ and go to heaven when they die. Yet they are anemic when they refuse to walk by faith, and are not ready for the impossible.

Abram and Sarai Tried to Take Charge

You can almost hear Abram and Sarai complaining, "Promises, promises. Where's the son of promise? Surely the Lord was playing a joke on us!"

Over twenty-five years before God had promised to Abram, "You are going to have a son." In Genesis 12:2 God promised Abram, "I will make you a great nation." But that was not at all likely. How could the seed of Abraham receive the land until Abraham had children? Abram and Sarai grew impatient during those years. In those days barrenness was looked upon as a curse. In my last chapter you read about Abram's listening to Sarai. The result was Abram's sex with Hagar and the subsequent birth of Ishmael, not the son of promise.

Like it or not God has made the husband the spiritual head of the home. Fathers and husbands, the devil is going to move right past you if He can, because God has made you the guardian of the door, the protection of your family. Sarai came to Abram and said, "I want you to have a child by Hagar." Abram replied, All right, I'll do that," and out of that union came Ishmael. You exclaim "That's sin!" Yes, it was. Abram failed in that moment in his family of faith. He listened to human voices, rather than to the voice of God.

Now thirteen years had passed after Ishmael's birth. God had changed Abram's name to Abraham (Gen. 17:5) and Sarai's to Sarah (17:15). When Abraham was ninety-nine years old God appeared to him and revealed that He was going to reaffirm the covenant that Abraham would still have a son by Sarah, his wife. Still the "son of promise" was to arrive, even though Ishmael had entered his teens. He was not the son of promise. Here we behold the *miracle* of faith and the *mockery* of faith. In these eight verses we are made aware of the miracle of faith. The miracle of Isaac's birth was again forecast in these verses, for notice:

"As the Lord had said..."

"The Lord had spoken."

Three times before God had already prophesied the coming of Isaac, the son of Abraham and Sarah. Only God can prophesy. Astrologers can make all kinds of noise. They can speculate, but only God can prophesy.

God prophesied to Abraham that Sarah would bear a son. He promised, "at this set time in the next year" (Gen. 17:21). And between nine months and one year's time, the birth of Isaac came to pass. Abraham was 100 and Sarah, ninety when Isaac was born. When God had told Abraham that Sarah would have that son (17:17) Abraham laughed. He asked, "How can I have a son when I'll be a hundred years old?" And he continued, "and how is Sarah going to bear a son at ninety years of age?" When Abraham laughed here, it was the hilarity of faith. He was laughing out of sheer joy. The promise God had made years ago was actually coming to pass. For Romans 4:19-20 reiterates that Abraham "was strong in faith, giving glory to God." Chapter 17 of Genesis (v. 1) states that when God appeared to Abraham, He asserted, "I am the Almighty God." So when Abraham laughed, it was in faith. His laughter came because he recognized God was the Almighty God. Abraham was rejoicing as the truth sank into his heart: learning for himself that what is impossible with humans is possible with God.

It Was No Laughing Matter, but She Laughed Anyhow

In chapter 18, Abraham had three visitors from heaven. They sat down and ate a meal with him. Then they inquired, "Where is thy wife?" Of course, Abraham knew exactly where she was. She had her ear glued to the tent flap. You remark, "Good grief, I don't believe that!" Well, look in Genesis 18:10. She was eavesdropping on all that was going on in that tent. One of the most unusual women I have ever known about! Again God promised the birth of a son. This time He promised where Sarah could hear, and she laughed. Abraham had laughed the laughter of faith, but Sarah laughed the laughter of total disbelief. She said, "Who me? I'm so old I can't possibly have a baby."

She laughed but not for long, because the Lord asked, "Why does she laugh?" (v. 13). In verse 14 God followed with, "Is any thing too hard for the Lord?" Now scared nearly to death, Sarah blurted out, "I didn't laugh." She lied to God. The Lord calmly and gently admonished her, saying, "Nay; but thou didst laugh" (v. 15). Aren't you thrilled that God is often gentle with us. Yes, we are going to reap what we sow. Yes, we are going to face the consequences of sin. Sometimes all God needs to do is convict us with, "You laughed." "You know you lied." Those were His words to her. In fact, her laughter began turning into godly fear.

In Hebrews 11:11, the text does not even speak about this moment of unbelief in her life. She was known as a woman of faith. It does not even refer to her counseling with her husband to have a child by Hagar, who was a victim of circumstances and probably not a believer in God. She gave herself to Abram because she was a servant and expected to obey. Abram and Sarai had failed to be proper witnesses to the young woman who came from a pagan country. Hebrews 11:11, though, states, "Through faith Sarah herself received strength to conceive seed, and was delivered of a child when she was past age, because she judged him faithful who had promised."

She quickly recognized that God was at work. She was no longer laughing. She was a believer. Her fear was transformed into faith. Then in Genesis, 21, there was fulfillment in the family of faith—the miracle of Isaac's birth. Isaac was promised, and sure enough he was born. Abraham was 100 and Sarah was ninety. In her excitement, Sarah exclaimed, "I have born Abraham a son in my old age." And the text goes, "And Sarah said, God hath made me to, so that all that hear will laugh with me" (21:6). Now all were laughing with them, not at them. There was jubilation in the house. The child of promise had come. All the doubts and disappointments of the past had vanished, and God had kept His word. *The miracle of faith.*

What kind of faith do you have? Could God be able to perform miracles through your life because you possess the kind of faith Abraham and Sarah exhibited in their lives?

Ishmael's Mockery

Not only was the miracle of faith recorded in Genesis 21, but there was the *mockery* of faith. It was the leftover consequence of what Abraham had done when he had gone into Hagar and sinned against God. When we are bull-headed and stubborn, when we bypass the Lord and do things our way, we fall into trouble. We are going to reap the consequences sooner or later. It will pain us deeply, filling us with regret because we know we have disobeyed God.

On the day that Isaac was to be weaned, Sarah saw Ishmael "mocking" her young son and probably her as well. Hagar had now become a believer. She had already fled the home in one instance and made it almost all the way back to Egypt. But God turned her around, and she came back to Abram's household. She dwelt there as believer, for God revealed Himself to her. But Ishmael, now about fourteen years of age, probably was not a believer in the living God. He had been circumcised at the age of thirteen, when Isaac was circumcised at eight days old. By the way, Abraham in his old age was circumcised at that time (see Gen. 17:26). It was a religious rite symbolic of faith. Religious rites are not enough. Abraham had faith Isaac would grow to be a man of faith. But what happened to Ishmael? Even though he had gone through the symbolism, even though he had the religious rite, even though he had been circumcised, his heart may never have changed.

Here is a story for all teenagers. Young people can be brought up in a godly home and still not change their hearts. His own mother had experienced the living God, but that meant little to him. Ishmael is a warning to all teenagers. He went through some terrible years. He tested his father's authority, challenged his beliefs. His father's old-time religion wasn't good enough for him. The devil will do all within his power to pull young people off on to the wrong track. Because Abraham had disobeyed God, there was a prevention of total commitment in his life, and he was going to suffer the results of it. The flesh-and-blood result of it was Ishmael, who was now making a mockery out of the promised one of God, Isaac, the true son of promise.

Is there a Ishmael in your life? Is there an obstacle there hindering you from being what God wants you to be? Is it the crowd you run with? You have intended to win them for Christ, but there is a possibility they are preventing you from living for Jesus.

Maybe your Ishmael is a habit. You are addicted to alcohol, drugs, gluttony, or pornography; you feel trapped and you can't get out. Alcoholics, for instance, tell themselves all the time, *I can quit anytime I want to.* That's the devil's advice of deceit, for they cannot stop by themselves. They have become addicted.

Maybe you have disobeyed God, young person, in your dating relationships, and that has become your Ishmael; or you are an adult, and spiritual pride could be your Ishmael. The Bible warns, "Let him that thinketh he standeth take heed lest he fall" (1 Cor. 10:12). People with Ishmaels in their lives are all over the world. They think they are standing, but someday they are going to trip up because they have lied to God.

"Pride goeth before destruction, and a haughty spirit before a fall" (Prov. 16:18). Spiritual pride is desperately dangerous. All too often people talk about what they have done for God and not what God has done in and through them. When you encounter a person living by faith, and without Ishmaels hindering their lives, you will hear them talk more about the sweet name of Jesus than about themselves. Abram's disobedience to God led to his allowing the birth of Ishmael. The consequences continue to this day. Notice Genesis 21:10: "Wherefore she said unto Abraham, Cast out this bondwoman and her son: for the son of this bondwoman shall not be heir with my son, even with Isaac." Sarah wanted Hagar and Ishmael out of there. The angel of the Lord foretold that Ishmael would be "a wild man" (Gen. 16:12). He became a wild man. But Hagar prayed, "Oh, God, will you bless my son, Ishmael?" Abraham prayed: "Oh that Ishmael might live before thee!" (Gen. 17:18). God honored those prayers. The descendants of Ishmael are among the richest people in the world. His people are powerful, and influential. He lives on today in the seventeen nations of the Arab world stretching from the Atlantic to the Persian Gulf. Astride rich oil reserves, holding the center of energy in the world, Ishmael is right there. And Ishmael has plagued Isaac for over 4,000 years. He was born out of the will and purpose of God. Even so, God promised, "Yes, I'll make him a great nation" (see Gen. 17:20). During the feast celebrating the weaning of Isaac, Ishmael "mocked" the whole deal. Sarah saw Ishmael's lips curl into a sneer. In the New Testament Ishmael is displayed as an illustration of the flesh (Gal. 4:29-30). The flesh always mocks the things of the Spirit. The price of total commitment is to send the Ishmaels out of your life. It was tough for Abraham to do absolutely what God wanted him to do.

Sometimes Putting God First Costs

It is a joy to live for Jesus Christ, but sometimes putting God first is painful. It hurt Abraham to send away that boy and his mother. Can you imagine what it was like? Abraham arose early that morning and gave Hagar bread and a bottle of water (see Gen. 21:14ff). Why didn't he give him more of the world's goods? Perhaps Abraham was afraid that Hagar and Ishmael would soon become victims of robbery and thievery if they had many provisions. I can imagine that morning as Abraham prepared to send out his first son, never to see him again. He must have hugged him and cried, "Oh, Son, I love you!" But God had declared that Isaac was the promised son. Abraham may have thought, *If I could just keep Ishmael around, if something happens to Isaac, Ishmael would still be here.* But God insisted on *no.* Isaac today is related to every Jew on the face of the earth. People ask, "Do you believe the Jewish nation is going to heaven as a nation?" No, I do not. I believe that every person, regardless of race or origin, must come to Jesus one at a time for the salvation of their souls. The Jewish nation is still the blood lineage of Isaac. The promise of God.

Today there is the problem of Israel and the Arab nations. We will have Isaac and Ishmael, and until Jesus comes again there will be constant turmoil (not only in the Middle East but around the world, because Ishmael was born and had to be sent away).

Waving Good-bye to Ishmael

Often we may have to say No to the flesh, no matter how painful it may be, but the price of total commitment is to go with God. Whatever Ishmael is in your heart, whatever hinders you from a close relationship to the living Lord God, is your Ishmael.

Are you willing to emulate Abraham in sending from your life the cause of stress and turmoil? Real commitment will cost you, yes, it will cost you heartache, hurt, and pain, just as it tore Abraham's heart to send that boy away. But that is the way of faith. Expel the Ishmaels out of your life and trust the true and living God as you walk by faith and not by sight. "For without faith it is impossible to please God."

> Trust and obey, for there's no other way
> To be happy in Jesus, But to trust and obey.
> —John H. Sammis

11.

Turning Your Back on the World

Hebrews 11:23-29

By faith he [Moses] forsook Egypt, not fearing the wrath of the king: for he endured, as seeing him who is invisible. Hebrews 11:27

By faith Moses, when he was come to years, refused to be called the son of Pharaoh's daughter; Choosing rather to suffer affliction with the people of God, than to enjoy the pleasures of sin for a season; Esteeming the reproach of Christ greater riches than the treasures in Egypt: for he had respect unto the recompense of the reward (Heb. 11:23-26).

Here is the continuation of the Faith Hall of Fame.

On this earth, we have our halls of fame, and our heroes have monuments built to them. It is extra special in sports to be named to the Hall of Fame. But when you come right down to it, there is no greater honor than to be inducted into God's Hall of Faith.

It's really not farfetched to ask, "Can I be in God's Hall of Faith? Could it be possible that my name would be written alongside the names of Noah, Moses, and others?" Your name can be inscribed for all eternity in God's Hall of Faith. You cannot make it because of your family, your fortune, or your feelings. You can do it only through faith.

We can please God only through faith. The Bible says in Hebrews 11:6, "Without faith it is impossible to please him."

Faith is not fantasy. Faith is not make-believe. Faith is not foolishness. Faith is not a fairy tale.

In Hebrews 11:1, there is a grand summation, "Now faith is the substance of things hoped for, the evidence of things not seen."

The word "substance" in the original language means "reality." Faith is the reality of thing hoped for, and that word, in the original Greek, literally denotes the "thing in which we can trust." Faith is the evidence or the proof of things not seen. Faith is not fantasy, not the make-believe, but reality.

A Faith That Touches All the Bases

More than one preacher has referred to the fact that we Christians need a "Sanforized" faith—it will not shrink!

> O for a faith that will not shrink,
> Tho' pressed by every foe,
> That will not tremble on the brink
> Of any earthly woe!
>
> Lord, give me such a faith as this;
> And then, whate'er may come,
> I'll know while here, the hallowed bliss
> Of my eternal home.
>
> —William H. Bathurst

All around us people do not understand that faith is reality. Faith is the reality of what we hope for, those things in which we can trust, and the proof of things not seen.

Faith is obedience to God's Word, regardless of circumstances and consequences. Faith is taking God at His word and living according to what He says. Faith enables us to understand what God does (see Heb. 11:3). Faith enables us to see what others cannot see and to do what others cannot do.

America has reached the crossroads of decision, and it is not a decision that can be made in the halls of Congress— neither can it be made in the highest court in the land. It is a decision which must be made individually in the heart of every American. Now is the day of our decision.

"Now is the accepted time; behold, now is the day of salvation" (2 Cor. 6:2). Napoleon Bonaparte believed that there is a crisis in every battle, a period of ten to fifteen minutes on which the outcome hinges. To seize upon that moment can spell victory, but to fail and lose that point in time could mean defeat. Shall we, the people of these United States of America, live by faith?

"By faith Moses. . ." Now Moses' parents made a choice for faith. It required faith for Amram, his father, and Jochebed, his mother, to put Moses in a basket and place him in the Nile River near to the site where Pharaoh's daughter bathed. After all, Pharaoh had ordered that all of the male babies should be cast into the Nile River. "By faith Moses, when he was born, was hid three months of his parents, because they saw he was a proper child; and they were not afraid of the king's commandment" (v. 23).

By faith, Moses' parents risked their own lives to save the child. What if they had been discovered disobeying the edict of the Pharaoh of the land? By faith they believed that even in Pharaoh's palace, Moses would be raised in the manner of the Lord rather in the life-style of paganism. By faith they let Moses go.

Little did they realize that one day Moses would stand before the Pharaoh of Egypt and demand, "God said, 'Let My people go.'" If the parents of Moses, on that occasion, had not let Moses go, the people of God might never have escaped the bondage of Egypt.

The princess of Egypt adopted the baby Moses, and he became the foster grandson of the mightiest man on earth. Now who do you think was invited to be the nurse to teach and to train little Moses in the way of the Lord? His own mother. As Moses grew to be a young man, the time had arisen for him to make his own decisions.

When our son, Chris, had his 21st birthday, We bought him a birthday card and a few other presents. And on that card I wrote, "Now you're a man full-grown, and you're on your own. Love, Dad."

His mother, not to be outdone, wrote on that same card,

after me, "You may be full-grown, with life to enjoy, but don't ever forget you're Mama's baby boy. Love, Mom."

Moses Had to Make a Choice

Moses was full-grown and faced a crucial decision. The Bible says in Acts 7:22, "And Moses was learned in all the wisdom of the Egyptians, and was mighty in words and in deeds."

The Hebrew baby had grown to be a prince of Egypt. He enjoyed the pomp, the prosperity, and the power of the wealthiest society of that day. He had an urgent decision to make. Moses had to decide whether to remain a man of rank among the Egyptians, or to renounce all of it in order to join his own people, Israel.

Hebrews 11:24 indicates that "by faith Moses, when he was come to years, refused to be called the son of Pharaoh's daughter."

He turned down worldly measure and treasure. Why, he might have become the Pharaoh. There is nothing wrong with lofty position, mind you, if God puts you there.

Perhaps God will raise some of you reading this book to the heights of prominence in America and in the world. The Lord could elevate you to be known by every person on the face of this earth. And if God does it, you cannot afford to be elsewhere. If God is in it, He will help you rise to the occasion. Respond to the Lord Jesus moving in your life. Don't let criticism get you down. Throughout the Old Testament, Hebrews rose to prominence in the governments of the world—a woman like Esther and men like Joseph, Moses, Nehemiah, and Daniel. There is nothing wrong with high position if God places you there.

Most people do not think they are important, and most are not prominent in the world's eyes. What is important, though, is for you to be what God wants you to be. No Christian is more miserable than the one who reviews his life and sadly confesses, "I denied what God wanted me to be. I refused. I failed God; when He called me, I responded with a no.''

When God spoke to Moses' heart and called, "Leave your rank, leave your worldly treasure," Moses replied, *yes.*

Years before it was God's plan for Joseph to utilize Egypt's power for the good of God's chosen people. God raised Joseph up to employ the power and prosperity of Egypt. Yet, it was God's plan for Moses to oppose Egypt's power for the same purpose.

Once there was a prestigious man, Baron Justinian von Weltz, who renounced his title, his estates, and his income to become a missionary to what was then Dutch Guiana. Today his body lies there in a lonely grave, and he is largely forgotten by the world. Yet, you can be assured that he is not forgotten by God.

As he prepared to go as a missionary, he testified, "What is it to me to bear the title 'well-born,' when I am born again to Christ? What is it to me to have the title 'lord,' when I desire to be rather the servant of Christ? What is it to be called, 'your grace,' when I, of all people, have need of God's grace? All of these vanities I will do away with, and all else I will lay at the feet of my dear Lord Jesus."

Moses "Lost All Ambition for Worldly Acclaim"

All through life I see a cross—
Where sons of God yield up their breath;
There is no gain except by loss;
There is no life except by death;
There is no vision but by faith.
—Walter Chalmers Smith

Moses, *by faith*, turned his back on worldly position. He refused tribute by the world's standards. He not only refused that, verse 25 stresses that he refused the pleasures of the world—"Choosing rather to suffer affliction with the people of God, than to enjoy the pleasures of sin for a season." He could have sprawled in the lap of opulent luxury. The life of an Egyptian prince was unsurpassed. Moses totally turned his back on the pleasures of the world.

Admit it or not, there is a certain pleasure in sin. No matter how religious and "righteous" you may be, you cannot deny there is worldly allurement in sin. The devil plans it like that. Unless you are careful for Christ, you could yield. Don't kid yourself.

I heard about a man carrying a basket over one arm. In the basket he had a pot of beans, dropping them on the ground, and following after him were pigs gobbling up the beans. Someone remarked, "That's a strange way to feed pigs." The man with the beans said, "Oh, I'm not feeding them exactly. I'm taking my pigs to the slaughterhouse." What a picture.

There's pleasure in sin, but it is only "for a season." Sin feeds personal pride. Sin momentarily satisfies carnal desires. It is always contrary to God, and it is always temporary and transitory.

If America continues to wallow in sin, if America determines we're going to live by pleasure and pleasure alone, that pursuit of pleasure is destined to fade—and America with it.

A. J. Gordon wrote that grand hymn, "My Jesus, I Love Thee." The hymnals have this phrase, "For thee all the follies of sin I resign."

But that is not the original version. He wrote, "For thee all the *pleasure* of sin I resign." That man meant what he wrote, and Moses did what he did by faith. He left worldly pleasures, realizing they were but for a season but keenly aware that Godly pleasures are forevermore.

Psalms 16:11 expresses it well, "Thou wilt show me the path of life; in they presence is fullness of joy; at thy right hand are pleasures for evermore."

Moses refused the worldly trappings before him. "Just say no" is the anti-drug slogan of the day. But that has always been appropriate. Moses knew how to say no. Since 1922 when it was discovered, King Tut's tomb has astounded the world. That tomb alone reveals the extravagant riches of Egyptian royalty. All of the wealth of Egypt was at the command of Moses.

But he wanted riches that would last for eternity. He wanted goods that moth and rust could not corrupt and thieves could not break through and steal (see Matt. 6:19).

David sang, "A little that a righteous man hath is better than the riches of many wicked" (Ps. 37:16).

It is not a sin to be rich, but it is a sin for the desire to become rich to be the driving force of your life.

Paul advised Timothy, "For the love of money is the root of all evil: which while some coveted after, they have erred from the faith, and pierced themselves through with many sorrows. But thou, O man of God, flee these things; and follow after righteousness, godliness, faith, love, patience, meekness" (1 Tim. 6:10-11).

If you work hard to God's glory and you become wealthy in the process, that is wonderful. However, if in God's wisdom He somehow keeps you poor, that's also wonderful.

Moses Identified with His Slave People

It should not matter as long as you are in the center of the will of God. It made no difference to Moses. For forty years he basked in the wealth of Egypt, but for the rest of his life, he forsook that wealth because it interfered with his obedience to God.

Become determined to lay aside every weight and every impediment that would hinder your relationship to God. Whatever stands in the way of your being born into the kingdom of God and doing the will of God, lay it down. One fairly recent gospel song goes, "I've laid down every idol, gave up ev'ry title." Be completely obedient. "Trust and obey, for there's no other way."

By faith Moses refused all the trappings of being a prince and probably a pharaoh. By faith he gave it all up to serve God. What a privilege! What an honor! God may not ask you to give up your possessions and position. He does want us to give up sinful pleasures. The song goes, "I have renounced all sinful pleasure." He may allow you to have some treasure. He may make it possible for you to have position in this world. Yet, you must be willing to give up anything or everything for Jesus' sake. It's up to God whether or not you keep it. But your prayer ought to be, "Lord, I'd give it up." Moses gave it up. By faith he forsook the frills of Egypt.

"Esteeming the reproach of Christ greater riches than the treasures in Egypt: for he had respect unto the recompense of the reward" (v. 26). Moses took his stand with a despised, persecuted people.

If you are a Christian, prepare to be ridiculed.

The Bible says, "Yea and all that will live godly in Christ Jesus shall suffer persecution" (2 Tim. 3:12).

If you are never suffering persecution, if you are never ridiculed or put down for your faith, it may well be that you are walking with the devil rather than God. If you live for the Lord Jesus Christ, the world will make it tough on you. That is the reason so many people yearn for return to Egypt. They are unwilling to suffer for Christ's sake.

Many men have gone overseas and fought face to face in combat, but find it difficult to face the mockery and ridicule of a few associates. Some people are bold Christians until they are mocked and laughed at, and then they choose to blend in with the world rather than to take a stand by faith on the Word of God.

How did Moses brace himself for sharing the affliction of a despised people? In verse 27 there is the explanation, "By faith he forsook Egypt, not fearing the wrath of the king." By faith. It is the great enabler.

Moses saw eternity through the eyes of faith. He beheld the unseen realities that would last and also the baubles before him that would perish.

In verse 26b the text states, "He had respect unto the recompense of the reward."

That word, "respect", in the Greek is derived from two words, *apo* and *blepo*. *Apo* means "from" and *blepo* "look," "to observe," or "to discern." *Apoblepo* means to look away from all else toward one object. So the phrase, "He had respect unto the recompense of the reward," indicates that Moses was able to make the "long look." He looked beyond this vale of tears. He was able to fasten his eyes on the rewards of God. What a perspective. He was able to behold the glories of heaven and the grandeur of the future. He recognized that those "unsearchable riches" were infinitely greater than all the riches of the present.

More Important to Be a Child of God

The reason the Christians conquered the pagan world was that they outlived, outthought, and outdied the pagans.   —Author Unknown

To him it was more vital to be a child of God than to be a grandson of Pharaoh, more pivotal to be right with the King of kings than to be right with the king of Egypt. All of these he understood by faith.

"For our light affliction, which is but for a moment, worketh for us a far more exceeding and eternal weight of glory; While we look not at the things which are seen, but at the things which are not seen: for the things which are seen are temporal; but the things which are not seen are external" (2 Cor. 4:17-18). "Eye hath not seen nor ear heard . . . the things which God hath prepared for them that love him" (1 Cor. 2:9).

Paul had the right impression: "For me to live in Christ, and to die is gain" (Phil. 1:21). "For me to live is Christ"—if you had to complete that sentence how would you do it? "For me to live is _____"—who or what would you put in the blank?

Would you put family? "For me to live is family." "For me to live is fame." "For me to live is pleasure." "For me to live is affluence." What is the burning ambition of your heart?

If you cannot say, "For me to live is Christ," you will have to end the sentence like this, "And to die is loss (not gain)."

In time the bony fingers of decay will pull down the monuments you have erected on this earth.

Your monument may be your youth, your family, your fortune, your feelings, or the perversities of this world. If so, it is all going to crumble. "And the world passeth away, and the lust thereof: but he that doeth the will of God abideth for ever" (1 John 2:17). Jesus Christ is going to live forever, and only the men, women, boys, and girls who have answered, "yes" to Jesus are going to have eternal life.

If you have not been able to assert, "For me to live is Christ," you will have to moan, for all eternity, "To die is loss," because your destiny will be hell, where you will cry out, "Oh, God, have mercy on my soul."

The account of the rich man Lazarus in Luke 16 makes it plain. "There is a great gulf fixed," and his eternal destiny was already established."

Jerry Vines, copastor of First Baptist Church, Jacksonville, Florida, once related a touching story of two little boys he visited in the hospital.

The cots had been placed side-by-side. One boy had a high fever, and the other had been badly mangled by a truck. That severely injured boy said to the other boy, "Say, Willie, I was down at the mission Sunday School, and they told me about Jesus. I believe, Willie, if you'll ask Jesus, He'll help you. They said that if we believe in Him, and pray to Him, then when we die, He'll come and take us to heaven."

Willie replied, "But what if I'm asleep when Jesus comes and I can't ask him?"

His friend, in that torn-up body, said, "Just hold up your hand. That's what we did in Sunday School. I guess Jesus sees it."

Since Willie was too weak even to lift up his arm, the other boy reached over from his cot, and he propped up Willie's arm with a pillow. During the night, Willie died, and when the nurse found him the next morning, his arm was still propped up.

Is your arm propped up this day? Have you answered yes to Jesus? Willie with his arm propped up saw clear to heaven.

Moses by faith saw Glory, and he cried out, "I'm going in that direction." If you could see even part of the glories of heaven, nothing would keep you from going that way. Positively nothing.

The reason people refuse Jesus Christ is because they don't take the long look, because they are seeing only with their physical eyes. They cannot walk by faith because they cannot see the glories of heaven. "How can I see it?" That's a good question.

Every human being on the face of the earth can see the glories of heaven.

You can see it as Moses saw it—by faith. It is so plain people stumble at it. Well, then by faith you're to follow Jesus. What can you do? Come to Him exactly as you are. Recognize that you are a sinner. Realize that all have sinned and come short of the glory of God, including you. There's no hope for heaven outside of Jesus Christ. Face the fact: without Christ, if you were to die this moment, you would go straight to hell, with no hope for heaven. It's time to turn your back on the world.

> Come, then, and join this holy band,
> And on to glory go,
> To dwell in that celestial land,
> Where joys immortal flow.
> Only trust Him, only trust Him,
> Only trust Him now, He will save you,
> He will save you, He will save you now.
>   —John H. Stockton

12.

About Faith: Forward March

Hebrews 11:27-29; Exodus 8:25:32; 10:8-10,23-29

By faith they [the Israelites] passed through the Red Sea as by dry land: which the Egyptians assaying to do were drowned. Hebrews 11:29

We as Christians have a great heritage. Abraham is the father of faith. In Hebrews there is a "roll call" of Old Testament saints, many of whom could be called the fathers and mothers of the faith. Everyone of the men and women who came to God in the Old Testament did so by faith, the same simple faith which was required when we asked, "Lord Jesus, I'm a sinner, and I ask You to save me. I trust you as God's Son and as my personal Savior." We have the joy and the enlightenment of living after Jesus was incarnate on this earth, after He went to the cross, after He rose from the grave. Today He lives at the right hand of the Father, and the Holy Spirit indwells us. The spirit of Christ will live in the heart of any man, woman, boy, or girl who will answer "yes" to Him.

I repeat: in the Old Testament, those who came to God did it by faith. Some believe they came by the law. Others believe they simply came by their good works. All of them approached God through faith.

Moses was one of those heroes of the Old Testament who knew what it was to live by faith. In Hebrews 11, beginning in verse 27, we read, "By faith. . . ." We quickly learn about Moses' faith. "By faith he forsook Egypt, not fearing the wrath of the king: for he endured, as seeing him who is invisible. Through faith he kept the passover, and the sprinkling of blood, lest he that destroyed the first-born should touch them. By faith they passed through the Red Sea as by dry land: which the Egyptians assaying to do were drowned" (Heb. 11:27-29).

Jesus tells us plainly that Abraham looked forward to His day and rejoiced. "Your father Abraham rejoiced to see my day: and he saw it, and was glad" (John 9:56). In the same manner, Moses looked forward to the day of Jesus. From then until now, fathers of faith have led us to Jesus. By faith many of them died for Jesus' sake. By faith they settled a new land called America. By faith they framed the Constitution of these United States of America. By faith they guaranteed our freedom, a freedom which men still try to destroy.

But they cannot destroy our freedom, for our forefathers saw to it that our nation is a republic. If we were a pure democracy today, the majority of America's people could vote to close the doors of our churches. Because we are a republic, our rights and freedom to worship are guaranteed by the Constitution of the United States. By faith men and women everywhere discover that "If the Son therefore shall make you free, ye shall be free indeed" (John 8:36). With tears in our eyes and thanksgiving in our hearts we are able to sing

> Faith of our Fathers, living still. In spite of dungeon, fire and sword. Oh, how our hearts beat high with joy. Whene'er we hear that glorious word. Faith of our fathers, holy faith. We shall be true to thee til death.

With Paul, many fathers of the faith could testify, "I bear on my body the brand-marks of Jesus" (Gal. 6:17, NASB).

Walking Away from Power and Prestige

Now I want you to see in this passage the view of faith, the verity of faith, and the vitality of faith. Notice in verse 27: "By faith he forsook Egypt . . . for he endured, as seeing him who is invisible." Moses through faith could see what others could not see with their physical eyes. He saw the Lord, as Isaiah saw Him, "high and lifted up" and on

His throne. Moses could behold the very glories of heaven. I believe Moses could see Jesus on His throne. Because he could see Him who is invisible, Moses made a crucial decision to lay down the royal robes of Egyptian rule and pick up the shepherd garment of a despised people.

"By faith he forsook Egypt." He did more than simply leave. He turned his back on Egypt, which had been precious to him. He renounced all it represented and renounced it permanently. He was never going back to it. Because of his decision, Moses faced Pharaoh, and Pharaoh intended to strike fear into Moses' heart. Fear is the most effective weapon Satan has, and he uses the weapon of fear against the people of God. Think about it.

We are afraid of being thought "different." Some are even embarrassed to bow their heads in public to pray, "Dear Lord Jesus, thank Thee for this food I am about to eat and the nourishment it brings, because I know everything comes from Thee." We are afraid of losing our job. We are afraid of losing our reputation. We are afraid of losing our popularity. We are often afraid of criticism from people whom we do not even respect, and yet Moses knew, as David knew and wrote in Psalm 27:1, "The Lord is my light and my salvation; whom shall I fear? The Lord is the strength of my life: of whom shall I be afraid?" So in spite of Pharaoh's wrath, Moses stood his ground.

Real faith will not fold under the pressure of fear. So Moses stood before Pharaoh, and he demanded, "God said, Let my people go." Now if Pharaoh had been wise, if Pharaoh had possessed knowledge and wisdom, he would have called out all of his chariots and instructed the drivers, "These people must go to a Land of Promise, and I want you to give them a royal escort." Pharaoh had no notion that every time you come up against God, you are going to lose. Pharaoh had the idea he could refuse Moses. So when Moses quoted the Lord God as saying, "Let my people go," Pharaoh was stubborn. The minute you begin to live by faith, you are going to have a head-on collision with the devil. If you live by faith and faith alone, you are going to find pain and suffering, affliction and difficulty.

The Devil Lures You Toward Compromise

William Jennings Bryan described a friend as having "no opinions—only convictions." Moses had rugged convictions.

Let's take an excursion into Exodus and ascertain what happened when Moses forsook Egypt. In Exodus 8:25, Pharaoh began to tempt Moses with compromise. Pay attention to Pharaoh's suggestion: "And Pharaoh called for Moses and for Aaron, and said, Go ye, sacrifice to your God in the land." What did Pharaoh mean? He was saying, "I want you to stay in Egypt. I want you to stay in the world system. Go worship your God. Make your sacrifices, but do your worship here in the world, in Egypt, in the land of darkness, in the land of compromise, in the land of bondage, in the land of slavery. Right here in the midst of darkness you should worship your God."

He was saying, even as the devil says to us when we come to Christ, "Why, you don't have to change many things. You just refine some of the things you already know." The devil whispers, "You just add a little culture to this thing called Christianity. But whatever you do, don't forsake the world." You see, when God calls you to be saved, the devil begins to insinuate, "Well, it's all right to have religion as long as there is no divine change, as long as there is no real repentance."

Some people claim to accept Jesus, but they never truly repent of their sin. They ask, "Lord, forgive me," but they do not turn around in obedience to God and promise, "I'm never going back into Egypt again." There is no true repentance. They say to Jesus, "I want the best You have, but I also want the best of the world." Jesus warned that you cannot serve God and mammon. Many want a religion of convenience with one foot in the church and one foot in the world. Pharaoh was saying, as the devil would say to us, "You can have your religion as long as you are in the world." The devil is not against religion. In fact, the devil is for religion, because he is aware that mere religion keeps people out of heaven.

Pharaoh, in essence, advised, "Stay in Egypt. Turn over a new leaf, but don't turn over a new life." Pharaoh was suggesting that there be no break with the world. Satan murmurs in people's hearts, "It is OK to be very religious as long as you are very lost." People in America do not need religion. They need to be saved from religion through the Lord Jesus Christ."

Pharaoh said, "Go ahead and worship your God, but do it in Egypt." And Moses replied, "Oh no! We are going to go. We're leaving this land." So Pharaoh argued, "Well, if you must go, if you'll not stay here, then stop in the wilderness."

Now consider Exodus 8:28: "And Pharaoh said, I will let you go" [as if he had something to do with it]. Pharaoh said, "I will let you go that ye may sacrifice to the Lord your God in the wilderness; only ye shall not go very far away: intreat for me." So Pharaoh decided, "If you are not going to stay in Egypt, then stop in the wilderness." But God did not want them to stop in the wilderness. God had promised a land flowing with milk and honey. Pharaoh said, "If you're going, don't go very far." The devil chides, "If you're going to be saved, don't be a fanatic. Just take it easy and make an excursion occasionally back into Egypt."

All of Us Must Experience an Exodus

All of us have a personal, spiritual Egypt, a point in our lives where we sojourn only until we can exit. We were never meant to stay in Egypt. If we make godly choices, as a result of *the* Passover, we will experience our own personal deliverance from bondage.

But God does not want us in spiritual Egypt. God wants us to be separate. "Wherefore come out from among them, and be ye separate" (2 Cor. 6:17a). When many people receive

Christ they stay so worldly they can't decide whether they are Hebrews or Egyptians. They never really depart from the world. They have enough religion to keep them from being happy in the world and too much world to keep them from being happy in Christ. They often stand there and tremble, miserable all over. Many have departed from Egypt, but they haven't entered Canaan. They have settled in the wilderness. That is a major hindrance to the church of God.

Pharaoh advised, "Stay in the world"—also, "If you're not going to stay, stop in the wilderness." God, because He has transformed our lives, is ready for us to be radiant witnesses for the Lord Jesus Christ. The reason so many Christians sitting in our churches are not witnessing for Christ is because they have either stayed in the world or stopped in the wilderness. They have confessed, "I believe," but there is nothing much in their lives to show they in fact believe that Jesus is the Son of God and their Savior and that they worship Almighty God.

God has called us to witness for Him. The problem with many churches is that they have too many leaders who will not walk across the street to share Jesus. Every leader in every church should be a witness, radiant in his desire to tell others about Christ. You inquire, "What's wrong with the churches?" We often have men who have been raised to positions of church leadership because of their business acumen, because of their community awareness, because of their high profile, because of their popularity or their personality. But a man ought first to be a man of God if he is going to help lead a church of any persuasion anywhere for God. The churches which do not raise men of God to places of leadership will become dying churches. Why? Because they are depending on men who have stopped in the world or in the wilderness, and they cannot survive that way.

Pharaoh had another question. Moses replied, "I'm going and I'm not stopping in the wilderness." "And Moses and Aaron were brought again unto Pharaoh: and he said unto them, Go, serve the Lord your God: but who are they that shall go?" Pharaoh concluded, "All right, you're going. You're going to the promised land, but who is going to go?" (see Ex. 10:8). Moses answered, "We will go with our young and with our old, with our sons and with our daughters, with our flocks and with our herds will we go; for we must hold a feast unto the Lord" (Ex. 10:9).

"And he [Pharaoh] said unto them, Let the Lord be so with you, as I will let you go, and your little ones: look to it; for evil is before you" (v.10). Pharaoh was warning, "All right, if you are going, do it, but it will be a dangerous pilgrimage." Throughout this confrontation Pharaoh tried to prevent Moses from taking all the people. The devil hates family religion. If the devil cannot keep you from being saved, he will try to keep your loved ones damned. When Moses, by faith, forsook Egypt, he carried his loved ones with him. Are you content to leave some members of your family behind? Can you honestly be content to go to heaven and let them go to hell? God commanded Israel in the wilderness, "Choose life in order that you may live and your descendants" (Deut. 30:19). At Shechem, Joshua declared, "Choose you this day whom ye will serve . . . but as for me and my house, we will serve the Lord" (Josh. 24:15).

Leading Our Loved Ones into the Family of Faith

The Philippian jailer implored of Paul and Silas, "Sirs, what must I do to be saved?" They gave the answer, "Believe on the Lord Jesus Christ, and thou shalt be saved, and thy house" (Acts 16:30-31). If he believed, the family would also be saved. They did believe, and the family was saved. That does not mean proxy religion, for the family also had to receive Christ by faith. If only we could sense a burden for our lost loved ones, then we would have a revival like we have never seen. So often we fear offending those whom we love the most.

Witness to a member of your family in a spirit of love. Do

not be sanctimonious with "piety" oozing. Your family members know better. But in all humility, in all seriousness, and in all love, go to your loved ones and speak with them. Also apologize if you have not properly lived the faith before them. Ask for forgiveness if necessary. Then tell them, "Jesus means so much to me, how I wish you could know Him as I do." Share the plan of salvation. If that relative would be offended, it would still be worth the opportunity you had to plead with them about Jesus. Don't leave your loved ones behind. We do not witness to them more because we are camped outside of Egypt. We are "playing footsie" with the world. If you are afraid of witnessing to a loved one, it is because the devil himself has struck fear in your heart. Pharaoh suggested, "Leave your family." Moses replied, "No. No, we're going. I'm going to the Promised Land. I'm taking husbands and wives, mothers and fathers, sons and daughters."

In desperation Pharaoh made one last stroke at compromise. In Exodus 10:24 Pharaoh suggested: "Go ye, serve the Lord; only let your flocks and your herds be stayed: let your little ones also go with you." Pharaoh finally said, "All right, you take your little ones but leave your flocks and herds."

The devil realizes that if he does not have your possessions, he does not have you, ". . . for where your treasure is, there will your heart be also" (Matt. 6:21). "It's all right to be religious," the devil hints, "just leave your business out of it." The devil does not want your wealth committed to God, but the Bible asserts, 'God owns it all" (see Ps. 50:10-12).

David exulted in Psalm 24:1, "The earth is the Lord's, and the fulness thereof; the world, and they that dwell therein." God does not want your money. He already has it! He owns the cattle on a thousand hills. Everything of which this earth is composed and every possession in our hands belong to God. They are already His. Tithing to God, giving 10 percent of your income to the glory of God and His kingdom, is not what you do for God. It is what God does for you. It is already His.

Sometimes I hear a person gripe, "I'm just aggravated. I'm not going to give my money to the church." That person has just cut himself off from the blessings of God! The people of God are to give to God. Some people give 10 percent and then pat themselves on the back, bragging, "Well, now I can use the rest of it for myself!" That is another word for Satan. You are just as responsible for how you spend the nine tenths as you are for the one tenth. If you go out and misspend the nine tenths you are being just as disobedient to God as when you fail to give the tenth.

How I pray that the next generation will walk in the faith of our fathers and that *you* will be named among those who are in the Hall of Faith. I pray you will lead your children in Bible study. I hope you will pray with your children and teach them the Word of God. We must have fathers in America who will lead their little ones, who will carry Christ into their businesses, who will direct their finances into the kingdom of God. We must have men who will admit, "Lord, I know everything I have or ever hope to have is Yours, and I know when I die that every last penny is going to stay on this earth. Oh, God, I give it all to You. Now teach me what to do with it."

Breaking Free of an Unsavory Life-style

Real commitment involves waving good-bye to Egypt—representative of the world system without Christ—and making a clean break. It's never easy. There is the constant temptation to look over your shoulder and even occasionally, for a fleeting moment, yearn to return for a visit.

Many people want to come out of Egypt, but they still want to leave certain baggage there. No one will ever have the vision of faith in their spiritual life until they are honest with God about their finances. You may remark, "I seem to be blessed of God," but you don't know the difference until you are obedient in your walk with God. You don't have an idea what you're missing. You can't be obedient partially. You must lay it on the line as Moses did to Pharaoh. In

Exodus 10:26a, Moses said, "Our cattle also shall go with us; there shall not a hoof be left behind." A man of God should tell off the prince of darkness, "Devil, I'm not leaving one dime to be used for your kingdom."

Moses spelled it out, "We are going. We are *all* going. We are all going *all* the way and, everything we have is going with us." What would happen if we did that today? You ask, "Well, how did Moses do it?" Remember Hebrews 11:27: "By faith he [Moses] forsook Egypt." He could stand boldly before Pharaoh because he saw by faith another King, an invisible King. When you see the Lord and fear the Lord in awe and reverence, you don't have to fear anybody else. By faith Moses endured.

In verse 28, there is the *verity* of faith. The tenth and last plague that God sent on the Egyptians was the death of all the firstborn (Ex. 11:5). To protect the Israelites from the plague, the Passover was instituted. Lamb's blood was sprinkled on the door posts and upon the lintels of their houses (Ex. 12:7). The blood was symbolic of Christ's sacrifice by which He conquered death for all that would believe in Him. God commanded it, and they obeyed. Obedience is essential.

They Wouldn't Bow, Wouldn't Budge, Wouldn't Burn!

Shadrach, Meshach, and Abed-nego had the choice of obeying King Nebuchadnezzar whom they could see before them, or obeying God, whom they could not see with their eyes. Without hesitation they obeyed God. They were bound and thrown into a fiery furnace. The king looked in and inquired, "Did we not cast three men bound into the midst of the fire?" (Dan. 3:24b). He continued, "Lo, I see four men loose, walking in the midst of the fire, and they have no hurt; and the form of the fourth is like the Son of God" (v. 25). Tremendous fear struck the heart of Nebuchadnezzar, and he yelled, "Shadrach, came forth. Meshach, came forth. Abed-nego, came forth." Nebuchadnezzar never called for the fourth man to come walking out of that fire! When we learn to obey, we are living by faith and walking by faith. You can pray from now until Jesus comes. You can weep and beg and cry, but until you rise from your knees and walk that prayer in faith and obedience, you have not understood what faith is all about. You are to stand before the world filled with the Spirit of God and determine, "With all that is within me I am going to be obedient to God and to His Holy Word." The verity of faith is obedience. There is also a *vitality* of faith.

"By faith they passed through the Red Sea, as by dry land: which the Egyptians assaying to do were drowned." When Moses and his people came to the Red Sea, they saw water before them and Pharaoh's army behind them. They cried, "Oh no, we're trapped, we fear for our lives." The people panicked, but Moses encouraged them, "Do not fear! Stand by. The Lord will fight for you while you keep silent" (see Ex. 14:13-14).

The promise of God's Holy Word is that He will fight for you. You can believe in Him. Sometimes we talk when we ought to listen. Sometimes we move when we ought to stand still. Other times we stand still when we ought to move. But the fact of the matter is this: if we commit our lives to obedience in Christ, He will teach us that the test of faith is trusting Him when all we have are His promises. They soon believed Moses' promise from God, and they watched the waters part that they might cross on dry land. Our faith is tested when the waters are rising higher in our lives and when the problems and difficulties seem to overwhelm us. But the Lord uses those extraordinary times for the pleasure of showing us His faithfulness, His love, and His power. Had the waters returned too soon all the Israelites would have drowned instead of the Egyptians. The people had no guarantee except God's Word, but His Word is more than enough. Faith takes God at His Word. Faith is the victory.

Do you genuinely take God at His Word? Or do you read this or that in the Bible, and the Spirit of God illumines it to your heart, but you may say, "Oh, but I don't know how that would fit"? Listen, all they had was the promise of God. God's Word is always enough to those who believe! By faith we see Him. By faith Noah built his ark while the world looked on and mocked. By faith Abraham gave the choice of the land to Lot and dwelt quietly in tents. By faith Daniel continued in prayer, although he recognized the lions were hungry. By faith the three Hebrew children refused to worship idols though the fiery furnace was white hot. By faith Moses forsook Egypt, not fearing the wrath of Pharaoh.

They all acted as they did because they believed. By faith Moses saw Him who is invisible. By faith we must learn that the invisible is better than the visible. By faith we must learn that the praise of the invisible God is better than the praise of visible men. Then and only then can you choose as Moses chose. For then and only then will you prefer God over the world.

G. Campbell Morgan preached:

There is one other thing to say. Faith proves the unseen things not for itself only but for other men. By your faith you demonstrate the reality of the unseen to the world at large. You bring the unseen things into sight by your faith. By the victory your faith wins, you prove faith and prove the unseen things to the man of the world. By your strength in the hour of agony, I come to believe in God more perfectly.[1]

Note

1. G. Campbell Morgan, *The Westminster Pulpit* (Westwood, New Jersey: Fleming H. Revell, 1954), 305-306.